palacios

The question of how best to retain individual liberty in the American democracy is at the heart of this vitally important volume. Here William O. Douglas gives clear, ringing expression to his views on the old, the new, and the possible abuses of those human rights which have long been considered immutably established in America.

In Part I, Justice Douglas discusses such pertinent matters as the philosophy of the First Amendment, the conflict between free expression and other community values, and censorship and prior restraint. He then goes on to consider "the right to be let alone" under such topical headings as The Right of Privacy, Loyalty Investigations, Religious Freedom, The Dignity of Man, and The Right to Defy an Unconstitutional Statute.

In Part III of this provocative book, Justice Douglas sounds an alarm at what he regards as an increasing encroachment of the military in civil affairs. Whether he is writing of this, or of restrictions on Americans' right to travel, or of gagging censorship, William O. Douglas' words are to be reckoned with.

publicly or privately supported.

Prepared by a joint committee of the Association of the Bar of the City of New York and the National Legal Aid and Defender Association, EQUAL JUSTICE FOR THE ACCUSED is a comprehensive analysis of the problem. The committee, made up of distinguished lawyers from all over the country, has studied the merits and defects of the various possibilities and made detailed proposals to improve the present situation, especially in the big cities where the problem is most acute.

The full report, and its suggestions, will interest private citizens concerned about equality before the law, as well as lawyers and public officials.

Equal Justice for the Accused

EQUAL JUSTICE
FOR THE ACCUSED

by

*A Special Committee of The Association
of the Bar of the City of New York*

and

The National Legal Aid and Defender Association

DOUBLEDAY & COMPANY, INC.
Garden City, New York
1959

Foreword

For more than twenty-five years I have been interested in the efforts in different ways in various parts of the country to assure competent representation in the criminal courts for those who cannot afford a lawyer. What I have seen has not been calculated to bring joy to the heart of a lawyer interested in justice and in the legal profession. For one of the few things which has been generally recognized is that the primary responsibility rests with the Bar.

As the years have gone by I have wondered how soon and by whom an accurate presentation of the constitutional and social needs would be forthcoming. All of us, members of the Bar and public alike, are grateful for *Equal Justice for the Accused*. It gains authority as the product of a diverse group which has thoroughly studied an important problem.

Three quite different methods for furnishing legal representation in the criminal courts to those who cannot afford a lawyer have been used. The first is through counsel assigned by the courts, generally without compensation for services and often without reimbursement for expenses. The vitality of this system has been amazing in view of the fact, as the report points out, that there has never been much to recommend it either in social principle or practical operation. Its life has probably been prolonged by the oxygen pumped into it by the New Jersey innovation of a rotation in assignments throughout the entire membership of the Bar. But even there it has been favored more as an education of lawyers in professional responsibility than as assuring a fair day in court to defendants. The report, as I read it, believes that the problem cannot be solved through the assigned-counsel method. I agree.

The report recognizes, and almost all of us would agree, that a preferable system is that of defender services offered through private legal aid societies or the like. The recent development in the number and quality of these services, although belated, is to be acclaimed. The great obstacle has been the expense—and that, of course, is not diminishing. Personally, I have never believed that sufficient funds would be available to make this system an adequate ultimate solution for most communities. Very few have disagreed with me.

The third approach has been the appointment of a so-called public defender—a lawyer selected non-politically for full- or part-time work and duly compensated for his services out of tax revenues. The efficiency of this system has been generally, but not

5

universally, acknowledged. Its development has been delayed by the outcry that it smacks of communism and leads to the socialization of the legal profession. Reluctantly I must admit that lawyers as well as laymen have visualized this hobgoblin. Happily this opposition is diminishing as recent decisions of the courts and the mounting pressure to demonstrate the soundness and workability of our American way of life impress the Bar and the public with the need.

The report brings the good tidings that a fourth system has proved successful in the few places where it has been tried. It is the so-called "mixed private-public system." Control is entirely non-political and shared by lawyers and laymen. Substantial fractions of the necessary funds come from both private and public sources. It is interesting that within a month a Bar association study in the District of Columbia has recommended this plan for adoption there. *Equal Justice for the Accused* concludes that "this dynamic system should be able in practice to realize its full potential and meet all of the standards essential for adequate representation enumerated in this report." To which I am glad to say "Amen."

HARRISON TWEED

Contents

PART ONE
*Representation of Indigent Defendants:
The Necessity, the Past, and the Present*

Chapter I
The Necessity for Representation

Chapter II
The History of Defender Systems

Chapter III
The Present Methods of Affording Representation

PART TWO

Conclusions and Recommendations

Chapter IV

Standards   56

Chapter V

Evaluation of the Various Types of Defender Systems   62

Note to Chapter V

Chapter VI

Recommendations   78

Introduction

One of the continuing concerns of the American community in general and the Bar in particular has been the problem of the defense of poor persons charged with crime. For many years this question has enlisted the interest and effort of some of the most distinguished members of the American legal profession. Indeed, the concern shown by the Bar, as well as by other segments of the community, for the plight of such defendants is a reaffirmation of a basic tenet of our democratic society and a demonstration of the fact that, as our society has grown larger and its legal problems more complex, the law has not lost sight of the necessity of protecting the individual. This report is a study of what has been done and what still remains to be done to achieve the goal of equal justice under law for the many who cannot pay for the legal services they need.

I

Our inquiry had its origin in preliminary work done in 1954–55 by the Committee on Law Reform of The Association of the Bar of the City of New York on the question of how defender systems function and what steps might be taken to render them more effective and to increase their coverage. It soon became apparent that the scope of this inquiry was beyond the capacity of a committee of busy lawyers unassisted by a research staff. Moreover, it was felt that the problem was of such importance that a national committee should be formed composed of members of the Bench, the Bar, and others who were concerned and interested. Therefore, it was decided that an effort should be made to obtain funds from a foundation to support the formation of such a committee and a comprehensive study by it of the subject of defender systems. In late 1955 The Association of the Bar of the City of New York and the National Legal Aid Association (the Association's name was changed to "National Legal Aid and Defender Association" in the fall of 1958) were the joint recipients of a substantial grant from The Fund for the Republic, Inc. for this purpose. As our work progressed, it became apparent that its scope was such that additional funds were required. The Fund for the Republic, Inc. was agreeable to supplementing its earlier generous gift by the additional amount needed to complete our study and finance the publication of this report.

II

By the end of January 1956 the Special Committee to Study Defender Systems had been formed to administer the Fund's grant and to undertake a comprehensive study of the representation of indigent defendants in the criminal courts. Its membership was in part appointed by The Association of the Bar of the City of New York and in part by the National Legal Aid Association. The list of the committee contained in this volume states the background of each member and shows the breadth of representation, both geographically and occupationally. As far as possible all sections of the United States were represented; the committee was composed not only of practicing lawyers and specialists in defender work but also of judges, a law teacher and corporate executives. Orison S. Marden, president of the National Legal Aid Association, and Allen T. Klots and Louis M. Loeb, presidents of The Association of the Bar of the City of New York during the course of this study, served as *ex officio members* of the committee.

By the middle of February 1956, the staff of the Special Committee had been assembled. The director of the committee's study was Kenneth R. Frankl, a graduate of the Harvard Law School and a former New York County Assistant District Attorney. The consultant was Arnold S. Trebach, lawyer and student of political science who was at that time studying at Princeton University and who is now teaching at the University of Tennessee. Miss Elaine M. Gorson served the committee and its staff as secretary.

III

The Special Committee held its first meetings in March of 1956 and made a number of fundamental decisions as to the scope and nature of its inquiry. The committee decided to confine itself to a qualitative study of the operation of the three systems through which indigent defendants charged with crime are represented— the assigned counsel system, the voluntary defender system, and the public defender system. Typical examples of each of these three systems were selected and it was agreed that field trips should be made by the staff for the purpose of studying each selected example at first hand. It was also decided that it would be most desirable to have informed persons meet with the committee from time to time to discuss their experience with and points of view towards defender systems. In furtherance of this program, the Special Committee had as its guests at various dinner meetings the following: Herbert W. Clark, San Francisco, member of the Council of the American Law Institute; Edward J. Dimock, Judge of the United States District Court for the Southern District of New York; David Du Vivier, Attorney in Chief of the New York Legal Aid Society; Frank S. Hogan, District Attorney of New York County; Miss Florence M. Kelley, Attorney in Charge, Criminal Courts Branch of the New York Legal Aid Society; J. Edward Lumbard, Judge of the United States Court of Appeals for the Second Circuit; Edward McConnell, Administrative Director of the Courts of New Jersey; Leland Tolman, Deputy Administrator of the First Judicial Department of the State of New York; Harrison Tweed, New York, past President of the National Legal Aid Association; and Arthur T. Vanderbilt, Chief Justice of New Jersey.

In its work the Special Committee endeavored to explore on as broad a front as possible the problems faced by defender systems in their practical operations. In this connection, the staff consulted with a large number of local officials, judges, practicing lawyers, persons affiliated with local defender systems, and others interested in defender work. We should like to take this opportunity to thank those who so very generously gave of their time so that the factual foundation upon which this study rests might be complete.

IV

In its work the committee was assisted and supported by a great many people. It enjoyed the interest and encouragement of President Klots and President Loeb. It always had the thoughtful and constant support and interest of President Marden, whose contributions to this report cannot be overemphasized. The staff of The Association of the Bar and the National Legal Aid Association were most helpful and the committee wishes to express its gratitude in particular to Mr. Paul B. De Witt, the executive secretary of the association, and to Mr. Sidney B. Hill, its librarian during the pendency of most of this study.

The work of Professor Bertram F. Willcox and Mr. Edward J. Bloustein of the Cornell Law School in making a field study and preparing a report on the assigned-counsel system of Tompkins County, New York, was of invaluable aid to the committee.

The committee also wishes to take this opportunity to extend publicly its thanks to the members of its staff who have contributed much to its endeavors and whose enthusiastic cooperation was indispensable to the production of this final report. I also wish to thank Miss Elaine M. Gorson and my own secretary, Miss

Jeanette Caso, for the many hours that they have spent in preparing the documentation from which the committee worked and
the manuscript of this report. Mr. Robert J. Geniesse, Mr. Melvin
H. Osterman, Jr. and Mr. David Sachs rendered a great service in
helping to check the final manuscript.

The committee should also like to express its gratitude to The
Fund for the Republic, Inc. for its generous financial assistance
without which this study would have been impossible. When the
study was begun it was understood that the committee was to
work with complete independence. This understanding has been
scrupulously observed by The Fund for the Republic, Inc.; the
Fund has not sought in any way to influence the course of the
study, to suggest appointments to the committee or to its staff
or to have any influence upon the committee's findings and conclusions. The Fund's only concern with this report has been to
provide the financial assistance required for our work. In all respects the relationship of the Fund and the committee has been,
from the committee's point of view, the ideal relationship between
a group engaged in investigation of a matter of public concern and
an educational foundation which has made the funds for such
investigation available.

V

The report which follows is based upon extensive field surveys
made by the committee's staff* and lengthy consideration by the
committee of the entire problem of defender systems. It is, we
believe, the first comprehensive study of defender systems.

The report is concurred in by all living members of the Special
Committee. It is with the deepest sorrow that I must note that
two members of the Committee died before the Report was com-
pleted—Judge John J. Parker and Mr. Thomas R. Robinson.
Their passing was a public loss; for us, who had worked so closely
with them on this study, it was also a deep personal loss.

As chairman of the Special Committee, I should like to record
here my deep personal gratitude to each member of the committee. All of them gave generously of their thought, effort and time,
often at considerable personal inconvenience. They joined in this
study because they believe that our democratic society needs to

---

*   *One field survey, that of Tompkins County, New
York, was prepared by Professor Bertram F. Will-
cox and Mr. Edward J. Bloustein of the Cornell
Law School.*

provide representation to all accused in order that the scales of justice can be equally balanced in every case. Their contribution here is another example of the American tradition of concern for the rights of individuals and the American desire to secure equal justice under law for all.

We present this study not only to the Bar and to the courts but also to all public-spirited citizens. It is our hope that the study which we have made will be but the beginning of a determined effort to support and extend defender systems in this country. If the report does this, it will have served its essential purpose.

ROBERT B. VON MEHREN

New York, New York
October 1, 1958

The Committee

ROBERT B. VON MEHREN, chairman—Practicing lawyer and partner in Debevoise, Plimpton & McLean, New York City. B.A. Yale; LL.B. Harvard. Chairman, Committee on Law Reform and member, Special Committee on Atomic Energy and Special Committee to Cooperate with the International Commission of Jurists, of The Association of the Bar of the City of New York; member, American Bar Association. Law clerk to Judge Learned Hand, 1946–47; law clerk to Justice Stanley F. Reed, 1947–48. Legal counsel to the Preparatory Commission for the International Atomic Energy Agency, 1957.

ROBERT D. ABRAHAMS—Practicing lawyer and partner in Abrahams and Loewenstein, Philadelphia. LL.B. Dickinson. Chief counsel, Legal Aid Society of Philadelphia. Vice-President, National Legal Aid Association. Founder and chairman, Neighborhood Law Office Plan of the Philadelphia Bar Association. Trustee, Dickinson School of Law. Lecturer-in-law, Temple University Law School.

BOUDINOT P. ATTERBURY, secretary—Counsel to James Talcott, Inc. B.A. Princeton; LL.B. Yale. Member, Committee on Corporate Law of The Association of the Bar of the City of New York; member, American Bar Association. Assistant United States attorney for the Southern District of New York, 1953–55.

EMERY A. BROWNELL—Executive Director, National Legal Aid Association and author of "Legal Aid in the United States," a report made as consultant for the Survey of the Legal Profession, 1951. LL.B. Syracuse. Member, American Bar Association, American Law Institute, American Judicature Society, National Association of Social Workers, International Bar Association, New York State Bar Association, The Association of the Bar of the City of New York, and Chicago Bar Association.

WILLIAM C. CHANLER—Practicing lawyer and partner in Winthrop, Stimson, Putnam & Roberts, New York City. B.A. and LL.B. Harvard. Member, Special Committee on Administration of Justice, Special Committee on the Courts, of The Association of the Bar of the City of New York; member, American Bar Association, New York State Bar Association and New York County Lawyers Association. Former corporation counsel, City of

New York. Former president, National Institute of Municipal Law Officers.

RAYNOR M. GARDINER—General counsel, Boston Legal Aid Society. B.A. and LL.B. Harvard. Vice-President, National Legal Aid Association. Treasurer and Director, Voluntary Defenders Committee of Boston. Chairman, William Underwood Company.

GEORGE NYE—Public Defender, Alameda County, California. B.A. Stanford. Member, State Bar of California, Alameda County Bar Association, and Lawyers' Club of Alameda County. President, California Public Defender and Legal Aid Association, 1951–52. Member, Citizens' Advisory Committee to the Attorney General on Law Enforcement, 1951–53. Member, Board of Directors, National Legal Aid Association.

ROBERT G. PAGE—President, Phelps Dodge Corporation. B.A. Yale; LL.B. Harvard. Instructor, Harvard Law School, 1925–26. Law clerk to Justice Louis D. Brandeis, 1926–27. Practicing lawyer in New York City with Root, Clark, Buckner & Ballentine and Debevoise, Stevenson, Plimpton & Page, 1927–47.

JOHN J. PARKER*—United States Circuit Judge; presiding judge, U. S. Court of Appeals of Fourth Circuit since 1931. A.B. and LL.B. University of North Carolina. Special assistant to Attorney General of United States, 1923–24. Alternate member, International Military Tribunal at Nürnberg 1945–46. Chairman, Section of Judicial Administration of American Bar Association, 1937–38; chairman, Special Committee of American Bar Association on Improving the Administration of Justice, 1940–47. Chairman, Committee of Judicial Conference of United States on Punishment for Crime, 1940–44; Chairman, Committee of Judicial Conference of United States on Administration of the Criminal Laws since 1952.

TIMOTHY N. PFEIFFER—Practicing lawyer and partner in Milbank, Tweed, Hope & Hadley, New York City. A.B. Princeton; LL.B. Harvard. Organizer, Voluntary Defenders Committee for Criminal Courts. President, the Legal Aid Society of New York, 1950–55. President, National Probation and Parole Association, 1937–41. Vice-President and Director of the Youth House, 1944–55. Trustee, Princeton University and Teachers College of Colum-

*　*Deceased*

bia University. Member, American Bar Association, American Law Institute, The Association of the Bar of the City of New York, and New York State Bar Association.

HERMAN I. POLLOCK—Practicing lawyer. Defender, Philadelphia Voluntary Defender Association. B.A. Temple University; LL.B. Pennsylvania. Chairman, Committee of Censors and member, Committee on Public Service, Committee on Criminal Justice and Law Enforcement, Medico-legal Committee, of the Philadelphia Bar Association. Member, Joint Medico-legal Committee of the Criminal Law Section of the Pennsylvania Bar Association. Member, Criminal Law Section of the American Bar Association. Member, Philadelphia House of Detention Study Advisory Committee. Member of Governing Board: National Legal Aid Association, Glen Mills Schools for Boys, American Civil Liberties Union, Greater Philadelphia Branch and Brandeis Lawyers Society.

THOMAS R. ROBINSON*—Public Defender, New Haven County, 1930–57. B.A. Catholic University; LL.B. Georgetown University; D.C.L. Yale. Member, American Bar Association, Connecticut Bar Association, and New Haven County Bar Association. Member, Board of Directors, National Legal Aid Association, 1954–57. Assistant Corporation Counsel, New Haven, 1918–26. President, Connecticut Exchange Clubs, 1932.

WOODSON D. SCOTT—Practicing lawyer, associated with Lord, Day & Lord, New York City. A.B. and LL.B. University of Kentucky; graduate fellow, Columbia Law School, 1927–28. Infantry unit commander, 102d Infantry Division, World War II. Member, Committee on Courts of Superior Jurisdiction of The Association of the Bar of the City of New York; Chairman, Committee on Legal Aid of The Association of the Bar of the City of New York, 1954–57; member, Committee on Aeronautics, New York County Lawyers Association; member, New York State Bar Association, Kentucky Bar Association, Federal Bar Association of New York, New Jersey and Connecticut and American Bar Association.

SYLVIA JAFFIN LIESE—Justice, Domestic Relations Court, City of New York. A.B. Barnard; LL.B. Columbia. Member, Committee on Socio-Legal Jurisprudence, New York County Lawyers Association. President, Wiltwyck School for Boys. Member, Citizens

* *Deceased*

Committee for Children and Board of United Neighborhood Houses. Assistant District Attorney, New York County, 1945–55.

HERBERT WECHSLER—Harlan Fiske Stone Professor of Constitutional Law in Columbia University. A.B. C.C.N.Y.; LL.B. Columbia. Member, The Association of the Bar of the City of New York and American Bar Association. Law clerk to Justice Harlan F. Stone, 1932–33. Special assistant to the Attorney General of the United States, 1940–44; Assistant Attorney General of the United States in charge of War Division, Department of Justice, 1944–46. Member, U. S. Supreme Court Advisory Committee on Rules of Criminal Procedure, 1940–45; Consultant on Revision of Rules of U. S. Supreme Court, 1953–54. Chief reporter, American Law Institute Model Code of Penal Law. Author: (with Jerome Michael) *Criminal Law and Its Administration* (1940); (with Henry M. Hart, Jr.) *The Federal Courts and the Federal System* (1953).

STAFF

KENNETH R. FRANKL, director—Practicing lawyer, associated with Liebman, Eulau & Robinson, New York City. B.A. and LL.B. Harvard. Member, Committee on Law Reform of The Association of the Bar of the City of New York; member, Committee on American Citizenship, New York County Lawyers Association. Assistant District Attorney, New York County, 1951–56.

ARNOLD S. TREBACH, consultant—Assistant professor, Department of Political Science, University of Tennessee, Knoxville. LL.B. Portia Law School; M.A., Ph.D. Princeton. Practicing lawyer, Boston, 1951–52. Member, American Political Science Association, Southern Political Science Association. Confidential investigator on Legal Aid to the Administrative Director of the Courts of New Jersey, 1955.

Summary of the Report

In presenting its report, the Special Committee to Study Defender Systems has sought to consider the problem of representing indigent defendants in terms partly historical and theoretical but primarily empirical. Its research was concentrated on the practical day-to-day functioning of the various systems which the American community has developed to meet this need. From this basis, standards for evaluating defender systems were developed. Each type of system was analyzed in terms of these standards. Finally, the committee has made specific recommendations for improving defender systems in general and for improving each type of system.

The report, which is summarized below, is divided into two parts. Part One, "Representation of Indigent Defendants: The Necessity, the Past, and the Present" sets forth the analytical and historical foundation for Part Two, "Conclusions and Recommendations".

Part One

Representation of Indigent Defendants: The Necessity, the Past, and the Present

Chapter I deals with the necessity for representation. It briefly develops the long-standing and continuing American concern for personal liberty and our insistence upon equal justice for all. It states the conviction of the Special Committee that justice cannot be equal and accessible for all unless every defendant brought into the criminal courts, irrespective of means, is represented by counsel.

Turning then to the issue of the necessity for representation, the report defines two elements of this necessity—the need of the individual and the need of society. The need of the individual may be summarized by these basic points:

1. The procedures of the criminal law are not easily understood nor readily mastered.

2. Soon after arrest and certainly not later than the preliminary hearing following arrest, a lawyer should be available to explain the charge, to investigate the facts, to prevent unreasonable detention and unjustified bail, to probe sympathetically for possible explanations and defenses, and to determine what course of further action the accused should adopt.

3. As the judicial process continues, a lawyer is needed to advise whether the accused should go to trial or offer to plead guilty, perhaps to a lesser charge, and, if the decision is to go to trial on a plea of not guilty, to undertake the complex of activities entailed in preparing for and conducting the defense.

4. In case of conviction, a lawyer should assist in connection with sentencing and advise whether an appeal is justified under the circumstances. If an appeal is taken, he should brief the case and present oral argument.

Turning next to the need of society, the report emphasizes that the concern of the American community with the requirement of fair trial is a reflection of its interest in fundamental human rights. It warns that, where society does not afford the right to defense counsel, judicial search for truth as we understand it is in danger. It is also noted that treating the indigent accused as fairly as any other group is essential to the proper administration of criminal justice. It should lead to greater respect for the administration of justice and should increase the chance of rehabilitating the guilty.

Chapter I concludes with a statement of the present chasm between the need and the satisfaction of the need. The committee maintains that many, perhaps most, of those defendants who have no counsel are unrepresented not because they elect to defend themselves, but rather because society does not supply them with counsel which they cannot themselves employ. The committee emphasizes that this is a matter of great public concern and one which requires public action.

Chapter II looks backward into the history of defender systems. It briefly tells the story of the struggle, both in England and the United States, to establish the principle that persons charged with crime have the right to the assistance of counsel and shows that, contrary to what is generally believed, the right of a defendant in a criminal case to retain counsel is a privilege of comparatively recent origin. The development of techniques through which indigent defendants who could not afford to retain counsel were given representation is then considered and the present state of the law with respect to both federal and state prosecutions is analyzed.

The report then considers the way in which systems to afford representation to indigent defendants have grown up in this country. It deals with the early growth of legal aid systems and their extension to the criminal field and with the early history of public-defender systems.

Chapter II concludes with a discussion of the causes of the growth of voluntary- and public-defender systems. It finds that the principal cause of growth was the fact that the assigned-counsel system could not cope with the problems created by the rapid urbanization of our country during the last eighty or ninety years. It develops the reasons why the assigned-counsel system could not be expected to work well under these new conditions and suggests certain reasons for the extension of legal aid into the criminal field and the growth of public-defender offices.

Chapter III considers the present methods of affording representation and is based primarily upon the accumulated experience of the members of the committee and the field surveys which were presented to the committee. The jurisdictions discussed are these:

1. *The assigned-counsel system*
   a. Essex County, New Jersey
   b. Tompkins County, New York

2. *The voluntary-defender system*
   a. Boston, Massachusetts
   b. New Orleans, Louisiana
   c. New York, New York
   d. Philadelphia, Pennsylvania

3. *The public-defender system*
   a. Alameda County, California
   b. Cook County, Illinois
   c. Dade County, Florida
   d. Fairfield County, Connecticut
   e. Hartford County, Connecticut
   f. Marin County, California
   g. The New Haven District, Connecticut

4. *The mixed private-public system*
   a. Monroe County, New York

Part Two

Conclusions and Recommendations

The Special Committee considered one of its principal tasks to be the establishment of standards which might be applied to evaluate the effectiveness of any system designed to afford representation to destitute persons accused of crime. It concluded that there are six basic standards which are of primary significance in evaluating defender systems. These standards are set forth in Chapter IV and are there discussed in detail. They are:

1. The system should provide counsel for every indigent person who faces the possibility of the deprivation of his liberty or other serious criminal sanction.

2. The system should afford representation which is experienced, competent, and zealous.

3. The system should provide the investigatory and other facilities necessary for a complete defense.

4. The system should come into operation at a sufficiently early stage of the proceedings so that it can fully advise and protect and should continue through appeal.

5. The system should assure undivided loyalty by defense counsel to the indigent defendant.

6. The system should enlist community participation and responsibility.

In Chapter V each type of defender system is evaluated in terms of the standards set forth above. This evaluation is approached from two points of view. First, is the system inherently capable of meeting the standard; and, second, does the system in practice meet the standard? In addition, in order to simplify the discussion, the six basic standards are grouped into three categories—the scope of representation, the quality of representation, and the community's responsibility. The first category is concerned with standard 1, the second with standards 2, 3, 4 and 5 and the third with standard 6.

With respect to the various systems the committee's conclusions are:

A. *Assigned-Counsel System*

    1. The Scope of Representation

a. *Although in theory the assigned-counsel system can provide the scope of representation which the committee believes to be desirable, it is extremely difficult for it to do so in most urban communities of the United States.*

b. *The New Jersey system is somewhat better designed to afford complete representation than the traditional system.*

2. The Quality of Representation

a. *The assigned-counsel system does not afford representation which is uniformly experienced, competent, and zealous.*

b. *The assigned-counsel system does not provide the investigatory and other facilities necessary for a complete defense.*

c. *The assigned-counsel system does not come into operation at a sufficiently early stage of the proceedings so that it can fully advise and protect and often does not continue through appeal.*

d. *The assigned-counsel system, at least in theory, provides for undivided loyalty by defense counsel to the indigent defendant.*

3. The Community's Responsibility

a. *The traditional assigned-counsel system generally fails to meet the standard of community responsibility.*

b. *The New Jersey assigned-counsel system comes somewhat closer than the traditional system to meeting this standard.*

B. Voluntary-Defender System

1. The Scope of Representation

a. *In principle there is no reason why a voluntary-defender system which has a sufficient staff and sufficient funds cannot provide the scope of representation which meets the local need.*

b. *Uncertainty and inadequacy of income are the major practical limitations upon the operation of voluntary-defender systems.*

c. *The scope of representation which a voluntary-defender system can afford may be limited by the physical arrangements of the courts.*

2. The Quality of Representation

a. *The voluntary-defender system can provide representation which is experienced, competent, and zealous.*

b. *The voluntary-defender system can provide the investigatory and other facilities necessary for a complete defense.*

c. *The voluntary-defender system can come into operation at a sufficiently early stage of the proceedings so that it can fully advise and protect and can also continue through appeal.*

d. *The voluntary-defender system provides for undivided loyalty by defense counsel to the indigent defendant.*

3. The Community's Responsibility

a. *A voluntary-defender system may perform the dual function of providing an institution through which the community's responsibility can be discharged and an instrument which may increase the community's awareness of its responsibility.*

C. *Public-Defender System*

1. The Scope of Representation

a. *There is no inherent limitation upon the scope of representation which a public-defender system can provide in the courts of its jurisdiction.*

b. *The fact that public-defender systems are created by statute makes it particularly important that provision for their improvement and expansion be made at the outset.*

2. The Quality of Representation

a. *The public-defender system can provide representation which is experienced, competent, and zealous.*

b. *The public-defender system is capable of providing the investigatory and other facilities necessary for a complete defense.*

c.   The public-defender system can come into operation at a sufficiently early stage of the proceedings so that it can fully advise and protect and can also continue through appeal.

d.   The public-defender system is capable of providing for undivided loyalty by defense counsel to the indigent accused.

3.   The Community's Responsibility

a.   The existence of a public-defender system indicates that the community has been sufficiently concerned with the problem of the indigent defendant to establish a public office and to appropriate public funds.

b.   The community must guard against the danger of believing that its complete responsibility has been discharged by creating a system and should continue to be concerned with and to support the system.

The committee also applies its standards to the mixed private-public system. It states that this system is close to the voluntary-defender operation in theory and in practice and concludes that it has great potentialities and should be seriously considered by communities which are either re-examining an existing defender system or seeking to adopt a new defender system.

In Chapter VI the committee sets forth its recommendations. Its basic conclusion, which affects all of its recommendations, is that in many places in the United States today justice is not equal and accessible for all. Therefore, its fundamental recommendation is that each community study the problem of the indigent defendant as it exists for it and take, as soon as possible, whatever action is required to provide adequate representation for him.

The committee then sets forth a number of specific recommendations which it divides into three categories. The first deals with recommendations of general application which are intended to aid a community in selecting the type of system most suitable to its character and its needs. The second category comprises recommendations which apply to all defender systems and are useful in that they should make it possible for any system to function more efficiently. The third is composed of those recommendations which make specific suggestions as to how each type of defender system might be improved.

A. Recommendations Relating to Choice of System

The committee's conclusions with respect to recommendations relating to the choice of a system are:

1. Any one of the recognized defender systems may be successfully employed in rural communities.

2. Because of the difficulties which the assigned-counsel system encounters in urban communities, any community with a population greater than 30,000 to 40,000 should give consideration to another type of system.

3. In determining what type of system is best suited to a community, consideration should be given to the number of indigent defendants within the community and, if the number of such defendants is relatively large in relation to the total number of defendants in the criminal courts, the community should seriously consider whether its needs can be effectively served by the assigned-counsel system.

4. The community must also, at the outset, consider the probable cost of the system and the community's capacity to meet this cost. Experience has shown that assigned-counsel systems in which an adequate fee is paid are generally more expensive than voluntary- or public-defender systems. If it seems unlikely that a voluntary-defender system can be supported through charitable contributions, the community may give particular attention to the establishment of a public-defender system or a mixed private-public system.

5. The community should also consider conditions within the local Bar. In particular, where a specialized Bar exists, it is unlikely that the assigned-counsel system will work well.

B. General Recommendations

The committee's recommendations relating to the organization and more effective functionings of all systems are that each type can be improved by the use of:

1. An advisory board which consults on administrative and policy problems, forms a bridge to the community and shields the system from undue pressures.

2. A panel of practicing lawyers which determines indigency where indigency is in question.

3. An annual report which keeps the public informed and solicits its support.

C. *Specific Recommendations*

The committee's specific recommendations relating to individual systems are:

1. *The assigned-counsel system.* The committee believes that the typical assigned-counsel system may be improved by:

   a. *Using rotation to assign qualified counsel;*

   b. *Centralizing assignment in a single administrative unit;*

   c. *Having indigency determined by someone other than the assigned counsel;*

   d. *Providing for the reimbursement of assigned counsel for all expenses incurred; and*

   e. *Compensating counsel adequately.*

2. *The voluntary-defender system.* The committee believes that a voluntary-defender system may be improved by:

   a. *Seeking the support of the practicing Bar through voluntary service by members of the Bar and by making use of law students attending educational institutions in the community; and*

   b. *Maintaining the quality of representation even if this can be done only by restricting coverage.*

3. *The public-defender system.* The committee believes that its recommendations concerning the voluntary-defender system apply equally to the public-defender system. It also concludes that public-defender systems may be improved by:

   a. *Securing enabling legislation which does not restrict the defender to service in particular courts, but permits expansion of the service as may be needed;*

   b. *Appointing the public defender and providing for his tenure in office in such manner as to eliminate or minimize political influences and other influences which might affect his professional independence and his loyalty to his client; and*

   c. *Providing an annual budget for the public-defender system so as to avoid case-by-case requests for funds.*

4. *The mixed private-public system.* The committee believes that the recommendations which it has made with respect to voluntary-defender systems also apply to the mixed system. The committee believes that the mixed system deserves careful consideration as one of the best solutions to the problem of representing the indigent defendant.

The report concludes, in Chapter VII, with "A Look Into the Future." Here the committee states its belief that the obstacles to the establishment of effective defender systems can be overcome within a comparatively short time. The committee concludes that the slight sacrifices required are fully justified by the worthiness of the cause to be served.

Part One

Representation of Indigent Defendants: The Necessity, the Past, and the Present

Chapter I

The Necessity for Representation

It is in the nature of man to seek justice, and the basic purpose of any good legal system is to provide it. One of the characteristics that has ennobled this nation and made it great is our insistence upon making justice equal and accessible for all.[1]

Among the many motivations that led to the early colonization of the North American continent, not the least was the search for a new land which would provide greater personal liberty than the Old World. When the colonies became a federal state, the Constitution of the new nation proclaimed that it had been formed to ". . . establish Justice, . . . and secure the Blessings of Liberty to ourselves and our Posterity. . . ." Throughout most of its history, the United States has been a haven for those who sought greater liberty. A continuing national concern for the rights of the individual has been the hallmark of much of its domestic, as well as its international, policy.

This national concern with individual rights has had its influence upon our legal system. It has led to that "insistence upon making justice equal and accessible for all" which Chief Justice Warren has rightly identified as one of the characteristics of America and one of the qualities which has made it great.

The Special Committee to Study Defender Systems is convinced that justice cannot be equal and accessible for all unless every defendant brought into the criminal courts is represented by counsel. In this first chapter of its report, the committee discusses the reasons why, if justice is to be equal and accessible for all, an opportunity must be provided by society for all accused, irrespective of their means, to have the help of an attorney. To do less than this is, in the opinion of this committee, inconsistent with the high ideals of our democratic society, which cannot tolerate one form of legal procedure for the rich and another for the poor.

The necessity for representation has two fundamental aspects—the need of the individual and the need of society. The individual defendant needs representation because he does not have the technical skills to conduct his own defense; nor can he be protected adequately by judge or prosecutor. Our democratic society needs to have representation provided to all accused so that the scales of justice can be equally balanced and the goal of equal justice under law achieved. After the need of the individual and of society has been demonstrated, the question naturally arises whether these needs are being presently satisfied. The final section of this chapter is devoted to a discussion of the present chasm between the need and the satisfaction of the need and states the considered opinion of this committee that much remains to be done before counsel will be available to all those who are entitled to representation.

A. *The Need of the Individual*

The need of the individual for counsel in a criminal proceeding is apparent to anyone who has ever observed such a proceeding. The procedures of the criminal law are not easily understood nor readily mastered. Most defendants need competent representation soon after arrest,[2] and certainly not later than the preliminary hearing following arrest.[3] At this early point in the criminal proceeding, a lawyer should be available to explain the charge, to investigate the facts, to prevent unreasonable detention and unjustified bail, to probe sympathetically for possible explanations and defenses, and to determine what course of further action the accused should adopt.

The need of the indigent defendant for a lawyer at this point is even greater than that of other defendants. In most cases the indigent cannot furnish any bail and must remain in jail pending disposition of his case, unable to help himself.

As the judicial process continues, the problems increase. Decisions may have to be taken as to whether it is advisable to request permission to appear before the grand jury; whether the indictment or information should be tested by a preliminary motion; and whether the accused should go to trial or offer to plead, perhaps to a lesser charge. If it is decided that the case is to be tried, counsel must undertake the complex of activities entailed in preparing for and conducting the defense. This may involve consideration of the advisability of waiving jury trial, the preparation of legal arguments, the search for witnesses, the cross-examination of the prosecution's witnesses,[4] and a decision as to whether to put the accused on the stand.[5]

In case of conviction, counsel must draw upon other skills which are also beyond the competence of the defendant. Automatic sanctions, which predominated in earlier historical periods, have been largely replaced by judicial discretion.[6] Today, in many situations, punishment to be appropriate must fit the individual as well as the crime. Consequently, counsel may be called upon to play a role in sentencing which requires wide knowledge and experience.

In the majority opinion in the landmark case of *Powell* v. *Alabama*,[7] Mr. Justice Sutherland summed up the need of the layman for counsel in these trenchant words:

Even the intelligent and educated layman has small and sometimes no skill in the science of law. If charged with crime, he is incapable, generally, of determining for himself whether the indictment is good or bad. He is unfamiliar with the rules of evidence. Left without the aid of counsel he may be put on trial without a proper charge, and convicted upon incompetent evidence, or evidence irrelevant to the issue or otherwise inadmissible. He lacks both the skill and knowledge adequately to prepare his defense, even though he have a perfect one. He requires the guiding hand of counsel at every step in the proceedings against him. Without it, though he be not guilty, he faces the danger of conviction because he does not know how to establish his innocence. If that be true of men of intelligence, how much more true is it of the ignorant and illiterate, or those of feeble intellect.

Recognition that the "science of law" lies beyond the layman's knowledge led, in part, to the constitutional and judicial development of the right to counsel, and of the right to be advised of that right. The presence of defense counsel is required by the adversary system which characterizes our judicial proceeding. The theory of the adversary system is that:

. . . each litigant is most interested and will be most effective in seeking, discovering, and presenting the materials which will reveal the strength of his own case and the weakness of his adversary's case so that the truth will emerge to the impartial tribunal that makes the decision.[8]

It was accepted as early as the fifteenth century that pleaders or advocates were necessary to aid each litigant in presenting his case.[9]

The contentious nature of the adversary system makes it impossible for the prosecuting attorney effectively to safeguard the interests of the defendant. Regardless of his fairness and the quasi-judicial nature of his office, the prosecutor must act as a protagonist; he cannot divorce himself from the part he must play and the duties he must fulfill as the advocate for the state. The unrepresented defendant cannot hope to meet the prosecutor's training and knowledge.

A layman is usually no match for the skilled prosecutor whom he confronts in the court room. He needs the aid of counsel lest he be the victim of overzealous prosecutors, of the law's complexity, or of his own ignorance or bewilderment.

These are the reasons why the right to counsel is "fundamental."[10]

Thus, the defendant without counsel is unable to avail himself of the benefits of the adversary system and the premise upon which that system rests is impaired.

The presiding judge cannot adequately substitute for defense counsel. No one can sit at the same time on the bench and at the counsel table. The difficulties involved have been emphasized by the Supreme Court of the United States:

> *But how can a judge, whose functions are purely judicial, effectively discharge the obligations of counsel for the accused? He can and should see to it that in the proceedings before the court the accused shall be dealt with justly and fairly. He cannot investigate the facts, advise and direct the defense, or participate in those necessary conferences between counsel and accused which sometimes partake of the inviolable character of the confessional.*[11]

Nor should undue reliance be placed upon the appellate process to correct convictions which may have been unfair owing to the absence of defense counsel. In this connection, it must be remembered that the unrepresented defendant is not in a position to make necessary objections on the trial, to decide intelligently whether to appeal, or to undertake an appeal effectively.

B. *The Need of Society*

The criminal law has been called "one of the most faithful mirrors of a given civilization, reflecting the fundamental values on which the latter rests."[12] In the largest sense, the concern of our society with the requirement of fair trial is a reflection of its interests in fundamental human rights. The concept of a fair trial includes, but is not limited to, matters of procedure. The rights which together define the concept of a fair trial—rights such as the right to an independent judge and the right to be heard—rest on a fundamental assumption of the dignity and worth of the individual and the fallibility of any single human judgment. Thus, the concept of fair trial is founded upon basic ideas from which the whole of democratic theory might be elaborated:

> *The right to assistance of counsel and the correlative right to dispense with a lawyer's help are not legal formalisms. They rest on considerations that go to the substance of an accused's position before the law. The public conscience must be satisfied that fairness dominates the administration of justice. An accused must have the means of*

presenting his best defense. He must have time and facilities for investigation and for the production of evidence. But evidence and truth are of no avail unless they can be adequately presented. Essential fairness is lacking if an accused cannot put his case effectively in court.[13]

Any society which does not afford the right to defense counsel gravely endangers judicial search for truth and risks its replacement by the purge or the ceremonial public trial.[14] The last decades have made us too familiar with both of these techniques. In neither of them is any balance, consistent with our ideas of morality and justice, struck between the power of the state and the rights of the individual.

The conclusion that the right to be represented by counsel is a most significant right in the protection of the individual is shown by many pages of history:

> *Sixteen centuries ago, Lactantius wrote, "Nobody is poor unless he stands in need of justice." It should give us pause not only that Magna Carta forced the king to agree, "To no one will we sell, to no one will we refuse . . . justice," but also that, in ancient pre-democratic days, many a Bill in Eyre or Bill in Chancery successfully asked the aid of the court because the petitioner was poor and needed help against a wealthy and powerful opponent. Surely our democracy should follow and enlarge upon those examples. Most of our state constitutions, echoing Magna Carta, proclaim that "every person ought to obtain justice freely without being obliged to purchase it. . . ."*[15]

Treating the indigent accused as fairly as any other group is essential to the proper administration of criminal justice. Citizens want to know that justice is done to all; their respect for the administration of justice will be increased by treating all defendants fairly and equally. Moreover, there is a greater chance of rehabilitating the guilty if they are prosecuted in such a way that they realize their rights are being respected. Obviously, unfair convictions do not encourage respect but instead create resentment in the convicted man and disturbing doubts in the public.

It seems clear that our democratic society has a deeply-rooted concern with the representation of the criminally accused. This interest should not be lessened simply because a defendant is economically unable to hire his own counsel.

C. *The Present Chasm between the Need and the Satisfaction of the Need*

It has been estimated that approximately 60 percent of those charged with crime cannot afford to employ counsel.[16] In many jurisdictions, this need for representation is not being met by any system. A recent survey made of 266 jurisdictions variously located in the United States resulted in the conclusion that "there is no adequate country-wide legal representation for poor persons accused of crime."[17]

In several states there is no voluntary- or public-defender system and the court is required to assign counsel only in capital cases. In several other states, assignment in non-capital cases is not mandatory.[18] Thus, the question whether counsel is to be assigned is left in many situations to the discretion of the court.

The necessity of having experienced counsel is so obvious that it is fair to conclude that many, perhaps most, of those defendants who have no counsel are unrepresented not because they intelligently elect to defend themselves, but rather because society does not supply them with counsel which they cannot themselves employ.

It is the considered opinion of this committee that this situation should be of public concern and requires public action. The one thing that our democratic society cannot afford to do, as Judge Learned Hand has reminded us, is to "ration justice".[19] Every citizen, therefore, should be concerned with the proper solution to the problem of providing counsel for the poor person accused of crime.

Chapter II

The History of Defender Systems

Although the necessity for representation is generally recognized today, defender systems have evolved slowly and have had to overcome many obstacles. Progress has been made but difficult problems still remain to be solved before the necessity can be fully satisfied and the ideal of complete representation achieved. However, before discussing the problems of the present and the future, it will be profitable to consider the past. Failure to do so would leave the reader without an understanding of the heritage of the various defender systems. And, without a glance backward into time, the substantive and analytical portions of this report could not be placed in perspective. Seeing the problems of today against the backdrop of yesterday should not only increase their meaning but also emphasize their importance.

A. *The Right to the Assistance of Counsel*

A résumé of the history of defender systems should properly begin with an historical survey of the right to the assistance of counsel. For, until persons charged with crime were generally permitted the assistance of counsel, there could, perforce, be no system for the representation of the defendant who could not afford to retain his own counsel.

The right to the assistance of counsel, as we understand it today, has two elements: the right to retain counsel; and the right, in certain situations, to have counsel assigned. The first of these elements is now so generally accepted that it is considered axiomatic. Indeed, it is sometimes stated that the right of a defendant in a criminal case to retain counsel is an ancient English common-law right. This is not correct. In common-law systems it is a privilege of comparatively recent origin which was recognized in the New World before it was accorded in England. The privilege came to be accepted as a right even later.

There is disagreement whether English law in the medieval period permitted accused felons to have counsel.[1] It is, however, undisputed that by the fourteenth century defendants were allowed to retain counsel only in minor cases. Persons accused of felony or treason were for the most part required to defend themselves, being permitted counsel only with respect to points of law. The harshness as well as the universality of this rule can be seen by considering one of the most famous treason trials of history—the trial of Mary Stuart, Queen of Scots. Her trial began at Fotheringhay on October 11, 1586. Two weeks later it was concluded at the Star Chamber and Mary was condemned to death. The sentence against her was carried out by decapitation on February 8, 1587.

At the beginning of her trial, Mary requested that she be permitted counsel. This request was refused on the ground that "forasmuch as it was a matter *de facto*, and not *de jure*, and altogether concerned a criminall cause, she neither needed nor ought to be allowed counsail in the answering thereof."[2] Thus, in full accordance with the laws of England, Mary was forced to defend herself before her judges on a capital charge in what was to her a foreign tongue.[3]

The first relaxation in England of this harsh rule was a statute of 1695 which not only permitted counsel in cases involving treason but also "authorized and required" the assignment of counsel to defendants accused of such crimes who requested counsel.[4] The next ameliorative steps were taken not by statute but by judicial grace. In the 1752 murder trial of Mary Blanding, the defendant was allowed to retain counsel who conducted both direct and cross-examination. And in 1755, McDaniel and other defendants, tried as accessories before the fact to robbery, were assisted by counsel assigned by the court.[5] Thus, during the eighteenth century, counsel was gradually permitted to perform an increasing number of functions for the defense. Sir James Stephen, writing in 1883, commented on this gradual relaxation:

> *From the middle of the eighteenth century to our own time there has been but little change in the character of criminal trials, and it is unnecessary to give further illustrations of them. The most remarkable change introduced into the practice of the courts was the process by which the old rule which deprived prisoners of the assistance of counsel in trials for felony was gradually relaxed. A practice sprung up, the growth of which cannot now be traced, by which counsel were allowed to do everything for prisoners accused of felony except addressing the jury for them. In the remarkable case of William Barnard, tried in 1758, for sending a threatening letter to the Duke of Marlborough, his counsel seem to have cross-examined all the witnesses fully, in such a way, too, at times, as to be nearly equivalent to speaking for the prisoner, e.g.: "Q. It has been said he went away with a smile. Pray, my Lord Duke, might not that smile express the consciousness of his innocence as well as anything else? A. I shall leave that to the Great Judge."[6]*

But it was not until 1836 that English defendants accused of felony were granted by statute the right to make their full defense by counsel.[7]

The grotesque law which denied counsel to those who needed assistance most was criticized by English commentators at least as early as 1758. Recognizing that the rule was settled at common law, Blackstone wrote: ". . . upon what face of reason, can that assistance be denied to save the life of a man, which yet is allowed him in the prosecution of every petty trespass?"[8]

For a variety of reasons, the English "rule was rejected by the colonies".[9] Many state constitutions, as originally adopted, contained provisions which made it clear that criminal defendants had the right to retain counsel.[10] In federal courts this right was clearly established by 1791 when the Sixth Amendment to the Constitution of the United States became effective. This Amendment provides: "In all criminal prosecutions, the accused shall enjoy the right . . . to have the Assistance of Counsel for his defense." And Zephaniah Swift, writing in 1796, could say of the Connecticut practice:

Our ancestors, when they first enacted their laws respecting crimes, influenced by the illiberal principles which they had imbibed in their native country, denied counsel to prisoners to plead for them to anything but points of law. It is manifest that there is as much necessity for counsel to investigate matters of fact, as points of law, if truth is to be discovered.

The legislature has become so thoroughly convinced of the impropriety and injustice of shackling and restricting a prisoner with respect to his defence, that they have abolished all those odious laws, and every person when he is accused of a crime, is entitled to every possible privilege in making his defence, and manifesting his innocence, by the instrumentality of counsel, and testimony of witnesses.[11]

Although the criminally accused were early afforded, in both federal and state courts, the right to retain counsel, it does not follow that counsel was appointed to represent indigent defendants who could not afford to retain counsel. In capital and other very serious cases, assignment of counsel to indigent defendants undoubtedly occurred on occasions. The first statutory provision for assignment of counsel to all indigent defendants was enacted in New Jersey in 1795.[12] New Hampshire had earlier provided for the assignment of counsel in capital cases only.[13]

Despite such early statutory recognition of the need for indigent defendants to be represented by counsel, today, more than a century and a half later, not a single state provides for the appointment of counsel to defend all indigents charged with criminal offenses, including non-indictable offenses. In non-capital cases, even though serious felonies are involved, there is no general mandate under the federal Constitution requiring the states to appoint counsel to represent defendants who cannot afford to retain an attorney.

On the other hand, the federal courts must appoint counsel for all indigent criminal defendants unless there is an effective waiver of this right.[14] Moreover, the due process clause of the Fourteenth Amendment has been construed to require state courts to appoint counsel in all capital cases,[15] and in those non-capital cases where counsel is necessary to assure a fair trial.[16] Some states, either by constitutional provisions, statutes, or judicial decisions, have made their state rule coextensive with that of the federal courts. Others, however, have not gone that far. Thus there exists great diversity in the practice of the several states and in many states a person can today be convicted of a non-capital offense in a trial in which, because of lack of money, he has been forced to defend himself.[17]

There is continuing judicial concern with this problem. The substantial number of cases decided in the last few decades by

the Supreme Court of the United States, as well as by the highest
state appellate courts, shows the degree to which this problem has
been subjected to judicial examination and the magnitude of
judicial concern:

*The substantial body of case law testifies that the counsel problem is
more than an academic one. It has vexed the United States Supreme
Court more than many of seemingly greater magnitude.*[18]

B. *The Growth of Systems to Afford Representation to Indigent Defendants*

Early America was characterized by an homogeneous population
living in rural areas. In this environment there was little need for
any system of representing indigent defendants accused of crime
other than assignment by the court on an *ad hoc* basis. For a long
time the casual assignment of counsel worked well. In the smaller
communities of eighteenth- and early nineteenth-century America,
most of the factors were absent which today may impede the operation of the assigned-counsel system in large metropolitan areas.
Thus, new approaches did not emerge until a changed environment created needs which the assigned-counsel system could not
adequately satisfy.

The nineteenth century saw successive waves of immigration
from the various countries of Europe. This gave impetus to the
developing urbanization of the United States and destroyed the
early homogeneity of the population. The needs of these immi-
grants led to the formation of social service organizations to assist
them. In 1840 the German Society in the City of New York was
incorporated, having been in existence as an unincorporated corporation for the previous twenty years. Its purpose was to assist
"German emigrants and to afford relief to other poor distressed
Germans, and their descendants."[19] In the same year the Irish
Emigrant Society of New York was incorporated. Its purpose was
"to afford advice, information, aid and protection, to emigrants
from Ireland, and generally to promote their welfare."[20]

Out of the German Society grew the first American legal aid
society, the Deutscher Rechts-Schutz Verein, founded in 1876. The
Verein soon ceased to be parochial in its choice of clients and
began to assist all eligible persons who came to it for legal advice.
It is the direct ancestor of the Legal Aid Society of the City of
New York.

It was from the metropolitan matrix of New York City that the
American legal aid movement sprang:

In the United States, legal aid started in 1876 also in New York City and spread from there to other metropolitan centers. To this day, legal aid is organized on a city, not a state, basis. Metropolitan influences have caused legal aid work to be organized in special offices devoted exclusively to the conduct of the work.[21]

By 1888 Chicago had an established legal aid system. Boston, Philadelphia, Pittsburgh, and Newark followed by establishing legal aid societies in the first years of the twentieth century. By 1916, thirty-seven American cities had some form of organized legal aid in operation. And, from its modest beginning in the latter part of the nineteenth century, legal aid has grown until by mid-1958 there were legal aid offices in 193 cities.

The legal aid movement entered the criminal field slowly, and for various reasons has never extended its activity in that area to correspond with its coverage in the civil field. By 1917 only one legal aid society was carrying on substantial work in the criminal field.[22] Today, of the 200 legal aid offices in existence by mid-1958, only six handle criminal cases.

Not all of the organizations representing indigent persons accused of crime and drawing their financial support from donative sources, however, developed as a by-product of civil legal aid work. Independent societies were established to supply counsel in the criminal courts, possibly because of the inability of the civil offices to meet the need for representation. There are now three such offices.[23] Since "legal aid" is a generic term, these private organizations in the criminal field generally have been denominated "voluntary defender" societies or organizations. This term has received such recognition that it is used in this report to include all private defender organizations, legal aid or otherwise, which are not governmental agencies.

Beginning in the second decade of the twentieth century, organizations grew up which were designed to serve the same purpose in the criminal field as had been served by assigned counsel and by legal aid organizations. These new organizations were called public defenders. The first such office was established in Oklahoma in 1911.[24] In November 1912, a new charter was adopted by the County of Los Angeles, California, which created the office of Public Defender. The Los Angeles Public Defender began operations January 9, 1914 and from that time has been a regular department of the government of Los Angeles County.[25] The early success of Oklahoma and Los Angeles prompted the establishment of a number of other public-defender offices. As of 1958 there were public-defender offices in over eighty jurisdictions.[26]

As they developed, both the voluntary- and public-defender

systems were faced with the charge that they were leading to the socialization of the Bar. Fortunately, this attack upon two techniques of meeting an urgent social problem did not have much effect. Both voluntary- and public-defender systems have grown, and the Bar still retains its independence and vigor.

It is the judgment of this committee that the charge of "socialization," whether leveled against the voluntary- or the public-defender system, is not only unwarranted but also obscures the essential problem. It is a charge laden with emotion and one which, in history as well as political theory, has no relation to voluntary- or public-defender systems as such. The charge of "socialization" would apply with as much force to many charitable endeavors as to a voluntary-defender system; with equal force to the public prosecutor as it does to the public defender. The charge has no meaning unless socialism is understood to encompass every device through which, by joint community activity or by an organ of the state, the community discharges a community responsibility. In this sense, all government is an aspect of socialization. Moreover, it is ironic that a charge which is sometimes intended to imply the exalting of the state at the expense of the individual should be levied against systems which grew up because of the recognition of the need for the individual to be protected against the state.

C.   The Causes of the Growth of Voluntary- and Public-Defender Systems

Some of the causes of the growth of voluntary- and public-defender systems have been hinted at in the preceding discussion. Of principal importance was the fact that the assigned-counsel system could not cope with the problems created by the rapid urbanization of our country which occurred at the end of the nineteenth and the beginning of the twentieth century. This was an era of dramatic growth. The population of the United States increased from about 40,000,000 in 1870 to approximately 92,000,000 in 1910.[27] Most of this growth was urban. As villages grew into cities, the volume of crime increased. An avalanche of criminal matters fell upon a system created to handle those of a rural society. This forced a re-examination of the administration of criminal justice and many urban communities recognized that the assigned-counsel system was no longer adequate.

In the early years of our history, the assignment of counsel to indigent defendants had worked reasonably well. In the small stable American community prior to the industrial revolution, more often than not, the defendant was known to the counsel assigned to him and, consequently, there was a basis for a good working relationship. The number of criminal cases was small and it followed that the burden of assignment was not heavy. Criminal trials were likely to receive great public attention and defense attorneys could ill afford to do less than an adequate job. Finally, and perhaps most important, the office of the prosecutor had not been specialized and the process of criminal justice was, on the whole, much less complex than it is today. Against the general practitioner turned prosecuting attorney for the occasion, the non-specialized assigned counsel could compete on even terms. The comparative simplicity of the cases made not only the trial itself more readily manageable but greatly simplified the investigatory aspects of the cases. In the days before rapid transportation, techniques for long distance communication, scientific detection, and the growth of organized crime, most criminal cases could be investigated and tried far more easily than the average assigned-counsel case can be investigated and tried today.

By 1919 it had become clear that the assigned-counsel approach could not cope with the representation of indigents in urban areas. In that year Reginald Heber Smith wrote: ". . . The truth about the assignment system in criminal cases is that as a whole it has proved a dismal failure, and that at times it has been worse than a failure."[28]

The failure of the assigned-counsel system to meet—particularly in the great urban centers—the growing needs of the indigent defendant created an environment in which new systems could evolve. That new solutions were tried is, at least in part, a reflection of the increased concern of our law during this century with the protection of the individual. As Dean Pound has said:

The problems of the last century gathered round the security of acquisition and the security of transactions. . . . In contrast the problems of the present gather round the interest in the social life of the individual.[29]

The direction which the new solutions took resulted from several factors. Since legal aid societies had been created to serve in civil cases, it was natural that some of them should undertake criminal representation as well. It was probably inevitable that the public defender—the counterpart of the public prosecutor—should also be tried.[30] With the 1929 depression, other factors came into play. The fear of violent social change may have reinforced the humane desire to see that justice is done to all.

As is so often true of legal history, the ferment and trends which had been observable for a long time merged and found their expression in a great cause. In 1932 the Supreme Court of the United States decided *Powell* v. *Alabama*,[31] and the majority expressed a belief which is still one of the cornerstones of all efforts to secure adequate representation for indigent defendants:

. . . [*the right to the aid of counsel is one of*] *those fundamental principles of liberty and justice which lie at the base of all our civil and political institutions.*[32]

Chapter III

The Present Methods of Affording Representation

Through its staff, the Special Committee to Study Defender Systems has directly observed typical examples of the means employed by various communities in the United States to afford representation to indigent defendants charged with crime. It has received and considered comprehensive field reports[1] on these observations. These reports divide into the following categories:

1. *The assigned-counsel system*

   a. Essex County, New Jersey

   b. Tompkins County, New York

2. *The voluntary-defender system*

   a. Boston, Massachusetts

   b. New Orleans, Louisiana

   c. New York County, New York

   d. Philadelphia, Pennsylvania

3. *The public-defender system*

   a. Alameda County, California

   b. Cook County, Illinois

   c. Dade County, Florida

   d. Fairfield County, Connecticut

   e. Hartford County, Connecticut

  f. Marin County, California

  g. The New Haven District, Connecticut

4. *The mixed private-public system*

  a. Monroe County, New York

This chapter, which describes each of these four systems, is based on these reports and a wide range of other information which has been considered by the committee.

A. *The Assigned-Counsel System*

The assigned-counsel system is still today, as it has been since its inception, the most widely used of the four systems. It is utilized in both urban and rural areas, and serves over half the total population of the United States—more than all the other systems combined.[2]

1. The Typical Assigned-Counsel System

The typical form of assigned-counsel system is found in Tompkins County, New York, and is characterized by decentralization, lack of co-ordination, and an *ad hoc* or case-by-case approach to its problems. The focal point of the system is the individual judge presiding over his court. When a defendant appears at the arraignment in the trial court without counsel, the judge may assign counsel to represent him.[3] Such assignments are made from members of the Bar qualified to practice before the judge and are generally made unsystematically. There is no system of rotation or any other technique to spread the responsibility of assignment evenly among the Bar. Counsel is appointed on whatever basis the assigning judge may deem to be appropriate.[4] As a general rule younger attorneys, who are willing to devote time to assigned cases in order to gain experience, are more frequently assigned than the experienced members of the Bar.[5]

Once assigned, counsel is under a duty to defend his client. Canon Number 4 of the *Canons of Professional Ethics of the American Bar Association* provides as follows: "A lawyer assigned as counsel for an indigent prisoner ought not to ask to be excused for any trivial reason, and should always exert his best efforts in his behalf."

In most instances, the assigned attorney must conduct the defense in a non-capital case not only without fee[6] but also without funds or facilities for investigation and preparation other than those which he himself may provide.[7] The responsibility of counsel assigned for the trial of a non-capital case generally does not extend to appeal. If there is an appeal, new counsel usually is assigned.

Counsel must be assigned in capital cases in both state and federal courts.[8] In selecting counsel for such cases, judges frequently call upon experienced members of the Bar to insure a high standard of representation. Most states provide compensation for attorneys representing an indigent person accused of a capital crime.[9] Some of these states allow the assigned attorney his expenses as well as a fee, whereas others limit compensation to a statutory amount—a limitation which may, depending on the work involved, result in a burden on the attorney. There is seldom additional compensation where an appeal is taken. In a few states, such as California and New York, counsel appointed to represent a defendant in a capital case are entitled to compensation for the prosecution of an appeal.[10]

2. The New Jersey Assigned-Counsel System

In an effort to improve the operation of its assigned-counsel procedure, New Jersey in 1950 adopted a distinctive and still unique system of assignment in rotation. The heart of the New Jersey system is found in Rule 1:12-9(a) and (d) of the *Rules Governing the Courts of the State of New Jersey*, which now read:

(a) Where a person charged with crime appears in any court without counsel, the court shall advise him of his right to counsel and of the privilege of having counsel assigned, if indigent, and assign counsel to represent him unless he elects to proceed without counsel or is able to obtain counsel. . . . Whenever practicable counsel shall be assigned before arraignment. . . .

(d) As far as practicable all assignments of attorneys or counsellors-at-law shall be made from the members of the bar practicing within the county in alphabetical rotation from a master list . . . except in cases of murder and where in the opinion of the judge the gravity of the offense warrants the assignment of special counsel. . . .

The principal difference between the New Jersey system and the typical assigned-counsel system is the introduction of a systematic technique of assignment. Under the New Jersey system, counsel are assigned in alphabetical rotation within each county, except where special circumstances are present, from a master list of attorneys practicing in the county. Each attorney is assigned infrequently, a typical attorney receiving an assignment approximately once in every three years.[11] Thus the burden of defending the indigent is spread among all members of the Bar—the convey-ancer and the corporate draftsman must take their turn along with the trial lawyer. This method reflects a basic assumption of the New Jersey system as well as of the traditional assignment system—that all attorneys have sufficient competence in the defense of criminal cases to represent defendants adequately. This assumption persists even though, in a particularly serious or complex prosecution, the judge may depart from the rotation practice and assign an attorney whom he considers to be especially qualified.

The New Jersey system also differs from the typical assigned-counsel system in another highly important aspect. Rule 1:12-9(a) provides that "[w]henever practicable counsel shall be assigned" before the defendant is arraigned in the trial court. One way in which the counties of New Jersey seek to implement this requirement of early assignment is exemplified by the practice of Essex County. There, shortly after a prisoner is committed to the county jail, he is given a form advising him of his need for a lawyer, making provision for a statement of financial condition, and containing a request that the court assign a lawyer to represent him without fee or cost. On the basis of the statements contained in this form, a judge of the County Court decides whether the prisoner is indigent and entitled to be represented by assigned counsel. If the judge concludes that the prisoner cannot afford to retain his own lawyer, a lawyer is selected from the master list and notified by mail of his assignment. The Essex County courts attempt to assign counsel within two weeks after arrest. Arraignment usually occurs some weeks later.

In post-conviction proceedings in New Jersey, the same attorney may continue with the case or another attorney may be assigned. Rule 1:12-9(c) provides that where an indigent person desires to appeal a conviction or utilize other post-conviction remedies, "the trial court or the appellate court on his application may assign an attorney or counsellor-at-law, as may be appropriate, to represent him." In practice, new counsel is assigned in many cases. For such new assignments the judge may select an attorney from the regular county master list, or he may request the services of the Habeas Corpus Advisory Committee. This state-wide committee processes special assignments to handle post-conviction applications by prisoners.[12]

B. *The Voluntary-Defender System*

Voluntary-defender organizations have been defined for the purposes of this report as private, non-governmental organizations representing indigent defendants accused of crime. They may or may not be affiliated with a civil legal aid organization. An example of one that is so affiliated is the Criminal Courts Branch of the New York Legal Aid Society.[13] The Philadelphia Voluntary Defender Association and the Voluntary Defenders Committee, Inc. of Boston have no such affiliation.[14]

The voluntary-defender system is characterized by what may be termed the "law-office" approach to the representation of the indigent defendant. While the assigned-counsel system generally results in a number of different lawyers being assigned from time to time to represent indigent defendants, the voluntary-defender system creates a law office which the court may assign to represent any and all indigent defendants.[15] These law offices vary in size from the substantial organizations of New York and Philadelphia to smaller offices such as New Orleans.[16] Nevertheless, under this system the function of defending indigents is centralized in a professional defense unit.

Voluntary-defender offices are privately controlled and supported. Private control is usually achieved through an independent governing body to which the staff of the organization is responsible. Financial support is sought either through independent efforts to secure charitable donations[17] or through participation in cooperative charitable efforts such as the Community Chest.[18] In some instances, both methods are used.

The voluntary-defender system may utilize trained, salaried investigators to assist its legal staff.[19] It may also be aided by volunteers from private law offices or local law schools.[20] The continuity of experience which a voluntary-defender office such as that of New York or Philadelphia represents, permits representation by veteran defense counsel even though the compensation which can be paid is generally less than that prevailing in private law offices in the same area.[21]

C. *The Public-Defender System*

The public defender, like the public prosecutor, is a public official. The former is retained by the government to fulfill society's duty to see that all defendants, irrespective of means, have equal protection under the law; the latter is retained by the government to serve society's interest in law enforcement. Generally, whenever there is a public-defender office, that office represents all indigent defendants in those courts in which the public defender regularly appears.[22]

Public-defender systems vary in size from large offices such as those in Los Angeles County and Alameda County, California, to a single-lawyer office such as the public defender in the New Haven District in Connecticut.[23] Some, such as certain offices in California, have facilities for investigation;[24] others have only limited funds and facilities.[25]

The staff of public-defender offices may be selected through civil-service procedures, appointed by the judiciary or the appropriate local officials, or elected.[26] On the whole, the legal staffs of public-defender offices appear to be relatively stable and in a number of instances these staffs have developed the characteristics of career services.[27]

The larger public-defender offices receive office facilities from the government.[28] However, smaller public-defender offices often are operated from the private law office of the attorney serving as public defender.[29]

Public-defender systems are financed by public funds. In some instances, they are treated in the same manner as other government institutions and submit a yearly budget to the proper appropriating body.[30] Others operate on a fixed retainer basis, the public defender being paid a yearly salary or fee for his services and being expected to finance his office expenses from his compensation.[31]

D. *The Mixed Private-Public System*

The cities of Rochester and Buffalo, New York, have a mixed private-public system which is unique in the United States.

Rochester has had for some time a Legal Aid Society which is active in civil cases.[32] In 1954, pursuant to an enabling statute,[33] the Legal Aid Society requested and received from the Board of Supervisors of Monroe County an appropriation to establish a defender service to function in the inferior criminal courts of the county. A lawyer employed by the Society has since performed this function.

Thus, Rochester furnishes counsel to the indigent defendant in lower court criminal cases within the organizational framework of a private legal aid society and supports this system by public funds. Buffalo has recently instituted a similar program of operation.

Although Rochester and Buffalo are unique in the continental United States, nearby Puerto Rico has an extensive criminal and civil legal aid system based on the mixed private-public concept.

In 1952 the Legislature of Puerto Rico gave impetus to the organization of the Legal Aid Society of Puerto Rico by providing that the Office of Court Administration "shall encourage the promotion of Legal Aid" with the co-operation of the Bar Association and the University of Puerto Rico Law School. Prior to the organization of the society, the only effective legal aid was supplied by five full-time public defenders, paid by the government, whose work was confined to the serious criminal cases in the larger cities. After the society was organized, these offices were abolished and their personnel were employed by the society.

The control and sources of funds of the Legal Aid Society of Puerto Rico reflect participation of the government, the Bar Association, and the public. The Board of Directors of the Legal Aid Society of Puerto Rico is composed of the Chief Justice, the Administrative Director of the courts, and the Attorney General representing the government. The organized Bar is represented by its President, the dean of the Law School, and another member designated by the President. Three laymen represent the public.

The same groups which exercise control provide the society's operating funds: direct appropriations are received from the Legislature; funds and facilities are granted by the Bar Association; and charitable contributions are received from the public.[34]

Part Two
Conclusions and Recommendations

Chapter IV
Standards

The Special Committee to Study Defender Systems considered one of its principal tasks to be the establishment of standards which might be applied to evaluate the effectiveness of any system designed to afford representation to destitute persons accused of crime. On the basis of its studies, it has concluded that there are six basic standards which are of primary significance in evaluating defender systems:

1. The system should provide counsel for every indigent person who faces the possibility of the deprivation of his liberty or other serious criminal sanction.

2. The system should afford representation which is experienced, competent, and zealous.

3. The system should provide the investigatory and other facilities necessary for a complete defense.

4. The system should come into operation at a sufficiently early stage of the proceedings so that it can fully advise and protect and should continue through appeal.

5. The system should assure undivided loyalty by defense counsel to the indigent defendant.

6. The system should enlist community participation and responsibility.

Each of these standards will be discussed in this chapter. In the following chapter, the various defender systems will be evaluated in terms of these standards.

A. *The System Should Provide Counsel for Every Indigent Person Who Faces the Possibility of the Deprivation of His Liberty or Other Serious Criminal Sanction*

This committee has concluded in Chapter I of this report that there is a need for the representation of all indigents facing serious criminal sanctions. Once this need is recognized, it follows that any system for affording representation to indigents should be of sufficient scope so that every indigent receives the aid of counsel. This definition of the desirable scope of any defender system is more than a logical conclusion drawn from a basic premise. It is also a recognition of the fact that the considerations of social policy which underlie the need for defender systems are not fully satisfied unless every indigent who is subjected to the possibility of criminal sanctions or the deprivation of his liberty is given an opportunity, irrespective of his means, to have counsel.

It is now generally accepted that there is a need for counsel in cases where the defendant is charged with a major crime. However, too little attention has been devoted to such need where minor offenses are involved. It has often been assumed that minor offenses do not entail serious punishment. This is not always true. In New York State, for example, misdemeanors may be punishable by an indeterminate prison sentence of not more than three years.[1] Moreover, most first offenders appear charged with minor crimes. If those first offenders who are too poor to hire their own attorney are left undefended, resentment towards the law for its apparent lack of concern may tend to reinforce the traits which have led to their first offense. On the other hand, the fact that the youthful defendant is afforded effective counsel may be highly significant in his early rehabilitation.

In addition to criminal prosecution, there are other proceedings which may involve the deprivation of liberty. While this committee has not concentrated its study on the scope and seriousness of these situations, it seems clear that ideally representation should be provided for all indigent persons whose liberty is in jeopardy.

The committee recognizes, however, that practical considerations may make it impossible to achieve, at the outset, the desired goal in all communities. The initial financial support may be insufficient to provide the full coverage desired. Consequently, any system should be planned so as to permit improvement and expansion.

Once a defender system has been established in a community, it tends to become a stable element in the local administration of justice. For that reason, unless the system is sufficiently flexible to permit improvement and expansion, it may be impossible either to extend the coverage of the system or to cope with the demands of the future without a basic structural alteration. It is always easier to change if the need for change has been foreseen and the system has been designed with the possibility of improvement in mind.

B. *The System Should Afford Representation Which Is Experienced, Competent, and Zealous*

Unless a defender system gives the indigent defendant competent representation, it is nothing more than a *pro forma* discharge of society's obligation to defend the indigent. Representation by inexperienced, incompetent, or unconcerned counsel cannot be considered to be adequate representation.[2]

It should, of course, be recognized that there are many lawyers without direct experience with the criminal law who are experienced in litigation and are qualified to defend many, and perhaps all, types of criminal actions. Moreover, to a certain extent, lack of experience in the criminal law can be compensated for by intelligence and diligence. Experience as an advocate is, however, essential. A recent comment by Judge J. Edward Lumbard shows its value:

A less experienced advocate might well have trimmed his sails to such a judicial wind as prevailed in the courtroom during this trial, and thus have jeopardized the rights and proper interests of a defendant on trial for a serious felony.[3]

This committee believes that any defender system which relies primarily on inexperienced members of the Bar is not providing the quality of defense which should be given. Younger and less experienced lawyers have a most important role to play but, at the outset, it should generally not be the leading role. They should be used to assist trial counsel and thus gain experience for further service.

C. *The System Should Provide the Investigatory and Other Facilities Necessary for a Complete Defense*

Experience, competence, and zealousness alone do not solve all the problems related to the defense of indigents. Facts must be investigated, time must be devoted to interviews and court appearances, and the opportunity to correct an unjust conviction through the appellate process must be available to the attorney.

One of the most serious problems faced by any defender system is the absence of proper investigatory facilities. This conclusion is supported by another recent survey.[4] In most criminal cases facts are the raw materials from which the defense is built. Unless the case turns upon pure questions of law, the defense cannot be adequately prepared without a thorough investigation of the facts. Although the task of defense counsel may be eased by the cooperation of the public prosecutor and the police, to prepare a defense properly usually requires considerable time and frequently necessitates substantial expenditures.

There are often many material facts which may be known only

to the defense and which may require investigation. For example, the preparation of a defense based upon an alibi may involve a time-consuming search for witnesses, documents, and records. Edward N. Bliss, Jr., chief investigator for the Los Angeles County Public Defender, in commenting upon the fact that the expense account of the Bureau of Investigation for this public defender is a revolving fund of $50 a year stated:

This, of course, prevents the investigator from attending many functions or locations where information may be obtained unless he does so at his own expense. Even investigations out of the county, wherein the defendant has given the names of witnesses residing in some neighboring town, or has cited certain incidents as having taken place in an adjoining county, are not provided for in the county departmental budget.[5]

The committee understands that this situation has been somewhat altered. The Los Angeles County Public Defender now has a larger revolving fund and travel outside the county is permitted with expenses, if not available from the revolving fund, being reimbursed to the individual who has incurred them.

In one of his last opinions, the late Judge Jerome N. Frank made an eloquent appeal for the provision of funds for investigation in cases handled by defender systems:

We still have a long way to go to fulfil what Chief Justice Warren has called our "mission" to achieve "equal justice under the law," in respect to those afflicted with poverty. In our federal courts, and in most state courts, there is no provision by which a poor man can get funds to pay for a pre-trial search for evidence which may be vital to his defense and without which he may be deprived of a truly fair trial. Furnishing him with a lawyer is not enough: The best lawyer in the world cannot competently defend an accused person if the lawyer cannot obtain existing evidence crucial to the defense, e.g., if the defendant cannot pay the fee of an investigator to find a pivotal missing witness or a necessary document, or that of an expert accountant or mining engineer or chemist. It might, indeed, reasonably be argued that for the government to defray such expenses, which the indigent accused cannot meet, is essential to that assistance by counsel which the Sixth Amendment guarantees. Legal Aid has no money available for that purpose, nor, in most jurisdictions, does the Public Defender (if there is one). In such circumstances, if the government does not supply the funds, justice is denied the poor—and represents but an upper-bracket privilege.[6]

In connection with the problem of investigatory facilities, it is important to note that, if the attorney conducts the investigation, he may later be called upon to act as a witness for his client. For example, the defense counsel who has also acted as investigator may have to testify to contest the credibility of a witness for the state who had made prior conflicting statements to him. Canon Number 19 of the *Canons of Professional Ethics of the American Bar Association* provides for this situation as follows:

> *When a lawyer is a witness for his client, except as to merely formal matters, such as the attestation or custody of an instrument and the like, he should leave the trial of the case to other counsel. Except when essential to the ends of justice, a lawyer should avoid testifying in court in behalf of his client.*

Any system, therefore, which fails to provide for a separation between the functions of defense counsel and that of investigator may force the originally appointed counsel to withdraw and require that new counsel be appointed.

D. The System Should Come into Operation at a Sufficiently Early Stage of the Proceedings so That It Can Fully Advise and Protect and Should Continue Through Appeal

The earlier any investigation is initiated the more effective it is likely to be. In fact, if the rights of the defendant are to be fully protected, the defense of a criminal case should begin as soon after arrest as possible. There is a strong argument that the time a defendant needs counsel most is immediately after his arrest and until trial.[7] During this period, unless the defendant has counsel, there is no one charged with the duty of protecting his interests and gathering the evidence which may be essential to his defense. The defendant, who is usually in jail, is incapable of doing anything to help himself and, while the prosecution is carefully building its case, the defendant's case may be destroyed by the mere passage of time.

It is the opinion of this committee that representation must be provided early if it is to be effective. This conclusion is not affected by the argument that the prosecution will be impeded by defense counsel in the performance of its duties. In a recent decision, Mr. Justice Black of the Supreme Court of the United States remarked:

> *It is undeniable that law-enforcement officers could rack up more convictions if they were not "hampered" by the defendant's counsel or the presence of others who might report to the public the manner in which people were being convicted. But the procedural safeguards deemed essential for due process have been imposed deliberately with full knowledge that they will occasionally impede the conviction of persons suspected of crime.[8]*

In addition to affording early representation, any defender system should make provision for the continuance of representation through appeal in appropriate cases. An appeal when grounds exist is an inseparable part of the process through which the individual's guilt or innocence of the charges brought against him by the state is established. Counsel is needed to assist with the determination of whether an appeal should be taken and, if an appeal is taken, to prepare and present it.

E. *The System Should Assure Undivided Loyalty by Defense Counsel to the Indigent Defendant*

The cornerstone upon which the relationship between an attorney and his client rests is that of the undivided loyalty of the attorney, within the framework of the canons of legal ethics, to the interests of his client. Unless the attorney is in a position to give undivided loyalty, and the client is aware of this, one of the basic conditions for the effective functioning of the attorney is absent. In defining the obligations of an attorney who has undertaken the defense of any individual accused of a crime, Canon Number 5 of the *Canons of Professional Ethics of the American Bar Association* emphasizes the distinction between the attorney's personal opinion and his role as an advocate:

> *It is the right of the lawyer to undertake the defense of a person accused of crime, regardless of his personal opinion as to the guilt of the accused; otherwise innocent persons, victims only of suspicious circumstances, might be denied proper defense. Having undertaken such defense, the lawyer is bound by all fair and honorable means, to present every defense that the law of the land permits, to the end that no person may be deprived of life or liberty, but by due process of law.*

Certainly, the attorney's obligations and loyalty to his client are no less when the accused is destitute and the attorney has been assigned to represent him.[9]

F. *The System Should Enlist Community Participation and Responsibility*

Implicit in a good defender system, whatever its form, is community participation and responsibility. The community is as responsible for the representation of the indigent person in the courts as it is for his treatment in hospitals and clinics. Lawyers may and should participate prominently in the management and support of the community's defender system but they cannot and should not carry either the full responsibility or the full burden. The organizational structure of every defender system should recognize the responsibility of the entire community and provide for the community's participation in the management and financing of the system.

There are a number of practical implications to these conclusions. Once it is recognized that the representation of indigent defendants is the responsibility of the community, the public interest in and concern with the entire process of the administration of criminal justice is increased. The problems of such representation are, as a consequence, less likely to be submerged among the many facets of the administration of criminal justice. If they are submerged, there is the possibility of support being withdrawn from the system or the system failing to serve society properly.

Therefore, this committee strongly urges that every community, in establishing a defender system or in reviewing its existing defender system, give thoughtful consideration to techniques through which the community's voice can be directly heard in the management of the system and the community's resources can be mobilized to support the system.

Chapter V

Evaluation of the Various
Types of Defender Systems

In this chapter each type of defender system will be evaluated in terms of the standards set forth in Chapter IV from two points of view: first, is the system inherently capable of meeting those standards; and, second, does the system in practice meet those standards. This dual approach may be of assistance to those communities which are reviewing their present systems in an effort to improve them and may also guide communities which may wish to change their systems. In both cases, it is important for the community to know the inherent limitations of a given system, and the practical difficulties the system is likely to face.

In order to simplify the discussion presented in this chapter, the six basic standards, which the committee concluded in Chapter IV were of principal importance in evaluating defender systems, have been grouped into three categories: the scope of representation, the quality of representation, and the community's responsibility. The first category is concerned with standard 1, the second with standards 2, 3, 4 and 5, and the third with standard 6. Each type of defender system will be discussed in terms of these categories.

A. The Assigned-Counsel System

1. The Scope of Representation

The assigned-counsel system is, in theory, capable of affording representation to each indigent person facing the possibility of criminal sanctions or the deprivation of liberty. However, in practice it is extremely difficult, particularly in metropolitan centers, for the assigned-counsel system to provide the scope of representation which this committee believes is required.

This is true both of the traditional system[1] and of the New Jersey system, although the latter appears better designed to afford complete representation than the traditional system. The rules governing the operation of the New Jersey system provide that, where an individual charged with a crime appears "in any court, without counsel," the court shall advise the defendant of his right to counsel and, if the defendant is indigent, of the privilege of having counsel assigned. Unless the indigent defendant waives his right to counsel or is able to retain a private attorney, the court is required to assign counsel to represent him.[2] As a matter of practice, however, indigent defendants appear to receive the assistance of counsel primarily in the New Jersey courts of original general criminal jurisdiction, the county courts. Assignments in juvenile and domestic relations courts and the inferior criminal courts, the municipal courts, occur infrequently. A recent "Report of Junior Section Committee on Indigent Criminal Representation" of the New Jersey Bar Association states:

Matters of a criminal or quasi-criminal nature are frequently heard in the municipal, juvenile and domestic relations and superior courts, and notwithstanding the availability of the right of counsel in most such cases, indigent defendants generally go unrepresented. In addition the present trend toward enlarging the jurisdiction and sanction available in the municipal courts coupled with the recommendations for the presence of a prosecutor in attendance therein will enhance the danger of conviction and subject the defendant to increased sanctions. The committee submits that some better practice of assigning counsel to these courts in such matters should be developed.[3]

In an effort to overcome this problem, a proposal has been made to establish a rotating panel of junior members of the Bar to appear on all arraignment days in the municipal courts.[4]

The practical difficulties which the assigned-counsel system encounters in providing representation in the inferior and lower courts of limited criminal jurisdiction are principally caused by the volume of cases handled by those courts and the speed with which these cases are processed. For example, in the Felony Part of the lowest court of original jurisdiction in New York County, the Magistrates' Court, there were about 14,000 general dispositions in 1955.[5] It has been estimated that, in at least 40 per cent of the cases in Magistrates' Court, the defendant cannot afford to retain counsel. The difficulties inherent in assigning counsel in more than 5,600 cases are obvious. Not only would the burden upon the Bar be tremendous but it seems inevitable that the processing of cases through the Felony Part would be slowed considerably. Primarily because of the volume of their business, the courts of lower original criminal jurisdiction in urban areas emphasize speed of disposition. Time would be lost waiting for assigned counsel to appear and to consult with the defendant. Many adjournments would be requested by assigned counsel so that they could attend to their private practice. The assigned-counsel system is hard-pressed to operate effectively in a judicial environment in which speed is considered to be essential.[6]

This committee has concluded, therefore, that, although in theory the assigned-counsel system can provide the scope of representation which this committee believes to be desirable, it is extremely difficult as a practical matter for the assigned-counsel system to provide this scope of representation in most urban communities of the United States.

2. The Quality of Representation

It is the opinion of this committee that the most serious defect of the assigned-counsel system lies in the quality of representation which it affords. The assigned-counsel system often fails to provide for experienced, competent, and zealous counsel, and for the investigatory and other facilities necessary for a complete defense. Moreover, it rarely comes into operation at a sufficiently early stage of the proceedings so that it can fully advise and protect and it often does not continue through appeal. Finally, while in theory the system should provide loyal representation, it does not in practice assure it.

(a) *The Assigned-Counsel System Does Not Afford Representation Which Is Uniformly Experienced, Competent, and Zealous.*

This conclusion applies equally to the traditional assigned-counsel system and to the New Jersey system:

New Jersey suffers with her sister states from the fundamentally objectionable aspects of the assignment system, namely: the inexperience of counsel, the inadequacy of professional resources and funds, the delay and loss of time and money in the inefficient and insufficient practice of criminal law.[7]

These difficulties are, in part, a reflection of one of the fundamental assumptions of the assignment system: that every lawyer is equally qualified to handle criminal cases. This assumption was largely correct in the smaller communities of eighteenth- and early nineteenth-century America. As long as the assigned-counsel system functioned in a predominantly rural society in which the practice of law was not specialized, the experience of most members of the Bar was similar and almost every attorney could be expected to have sufficient knowledge of criminal practice to prepare and present an adequate defense. With the growth of the city, the development of the large business corporation and the resulting specialization of legal practice, however, this assumption became invalid at least with respect to the larger centers of population.

This committee is of the opinion that there are today practicing in large metropolitan centers many lawyers who have had little or no experience in the trial of criminal or civil cases, and, as a consequence, are not qualified adequately to represent persons charged with crime.[8] This committee recognizes, of course, the many cases in which assigned counsel have presented defenses which were of the highest quality. But it cannot be ignored that, in most criminal cases, counsel without the necessary criminal or litigation experience are at a decided disadvantage which may adversely affect the quality of their representation. The extent to which the assigned-counsel system fails to afford experienced and competent representation is shown by a consideration of the operation of the system in Essex County, New Jersey, and Tompkins County, New York. Surveys of these jurisdictions show that in Essex County 43.4 per cent and in Tompkins County 33.3 per cent of the assigned counsel had no criminal-law experience before their first assignment.[9]

This defect of the assigned-counsel system appears to be inherent in the system. On many occasions assigned counsel have made excellent defenses, but the system cannot assure that result. In the judgment of this committee, this defect is not adequately compensated for by the fact that the assigned-counsel system provides a technique through which the recent law school graduate can be given experience in the criminal law. The purpose of affording defense to indigent persons is not to train young lawyers but to provide a competent defense.

Even if a particular effort is made to assign experienced and highly qualified attorneys to those cases involving serious felonies, this defect is not overcome. The defense of a relatively minor crime may be as difficult as the defense of a serious crime. The defense in both situations is important in the judgment of this committee since it believes that every indigent defendant should be afforded a capable defense. Under the assigned-counsel system, the only way in which this standard can be met would be to limit assignments to that section of the Bar which is experienced and qualified in criminal litigation. In many communities this solution would place an unjustified burden upon a small segment of the Bar.

(b) *The Assigned-Counsel System Does Not Provide the Investigatory and Other Facilities Necessary for a Complete Defense.*

This committee is of the opinion that neither the traditional assigned-counsel system nor the New Jersey system is able to provide the investigatory and other facilities necessary for a complete defense. Since assigned-counsel systems almost never provide sufficient funds or other facilities for investigation and the burden of investigating and preparing the assigned case usually rests entirely upon the shoulders of the assigned counsel, it would be almost miraculous if detailed investigations of fact were made in each case where such an investigation was necessary.

It is true that some assigned-counsel systems have attempted to meet this deficiency by use of law students to aid in the factual and legal preparation of the assigned attorney. However, the survey conducted by this committee's staff in Essex County, New Jersey, where this device is used, shows that the help received from law students—depending as it does on the student's interest, experience and academic schedule—is insufficient to meet the need for investigatory and other facilities.

(c) *The Assigned-Counsel System Does Not Come into Operation at a Sufficiently Early Stage of the Proceedings so That It Can Fully Advise and Protect and Often Does Not Continue Through Appeal.*

It is theoretically possible for the assigned-counsel system to come into operation as early as any other system. However, as a general rule, the assigned-counsel system does not come into operation until the defendant is arraigned after an indictment or information has been filed in the trial court. Therefore, in practice, the assigned-counsel system does not afford representation early enough to meet this committee's standard of timeliness. For example, the survey of the assigned-counsel system in Tompkins County, New York conducted for this committee, indicates that indigent defendants in jail often do not receive an attorney's aid for as much as three months after arrest.[10] The principal cause is that the Grand Jury meets only three times a year and counsel are assigned only after indictment. A survey conducted in New Jersey in 1955 under the auspices of the Administrative Office of the New Jersey Courts leads to the same conclusion. It indicates that in jail cases the estimated time between arrest and the first contact between the indigent accused and the assigned counsel is sometimes as long as 180 days.[11] New Jersey has recognized this problem, however, and a recent amendment to the rules governing the assignment of counsel in that state provides that "wherever practicable counsel shall be assigned before arraignment."[12]

Moreover, the assigned-counsel system, as a general rule, does not continue through appeal. This defect has been dealt with by the New Jersey system,[13] and it does not appear to be inherent even in the traditional assigned-counsel system. However, as a practical matter the representation afforded by the traditional assigned-counsel system too often ends at the conclusion of the proceedings in the trial court.

(d) *The Assigned-Counsel System, at Least in Theory, Provides for Undivided Loyalty by Defense Counsel to the Indigent Defendant.*

In theory the assigned counsel is in a position where he can be completely loyal to his client and in many cases the assigned counsel complies with the highest ethical standards in his representation of his client.

However, the fact that an assigned counsel is usually not sufficiently compensated for his services or disbursements puts economic pressure on him to dispose of his assignment with as little investigation and as hastily as possible. Moreover, where the assigned counsel is compensated directly or relies upon the judiciary for indirect compensation through, for example, appointment as a guardian or a trustee, the quality of his representation may be affected. Rightly or wrongly, he may believe that his conduct of the defense will influence future appointments.

3. The Community's Responsibility

The traditional assigned-counsel system generally fails, in the judgment of this committee, to meet the standard of community responsibility. In most jurisdictions in which the system operates, the general public is unconcerned with its operation and unaware of the problem of the defense of the indigent. Many members of the Bar are also unconcerned and unaware. This is particularly true in the larger metropolitan areas in which the assigned-counsel system is found. Many members of the Bar practicing in such communities are never assigned and have little interest in the operations of the assigned-counsel system in their community.

Where the assigned-counsel system is used, the defense of the indigent is necessarily scattered among the individual members of the Bar. This has two consequences. It tends to diminish community interest in the problems of the defense of the indigent because there is no central organization on which interest can be focused. It also makes it difficult for any general community movement seeking to improve or expand the defense of the indigent to be effective. This is particularly true because any real improvement in an assigned-counsel system is likely to require extensive structural change, for example, the adoption of the New Jersey system.

The New Jersey assigned-counsel system, in the judgment of this committee, comes somewhat closer than the traditional system to meeting the standards of community responsibility. At the very least, the New Jersey system should create an awareness of the problem of defending the indigent among the entire Bar because it requires a large percentage of the practicing attorneys, at more or less regular intervals, to represent indigents in the criminal courts.[14] Chief Justice Vanderbilt has commented upon the effect of this:

> Yet who can deny that in the long run the protection of our private rights and property rights depends in each locality on the adequate enforcement of the criminal law? And how can we expect the better grade of lawyers to have any interest in a field of which they have no firsthand knowledge? The great virtue of the New Jersey plan, as I see it, is that it gives every member of the bar some degree of awareness of the momentous problems involved in the enforcement of the criminal law.[15]

B. *The Voluntary-Defender System*

1. The Scope of Representation

In principle there is no reason why a voluntary-defender system which has a sufficient staff and sufficient funds cannot provide the scope of representation desired by this committee. This system is inherently flexible and need not be stopped by jurisdictional boundaries which conform to political divisions. Thus, for example, the voluntary-defender systems of Boston, Philadelphia, and New York provide service in the federal courts as well as in the state courts. However, all voluntary-defender offices examined by this committee have been unable in varying degrees to provide the extent of service which this committee feels is necessary.[16]

Uncertainty and inadequacy of income are the major practical limitations upon the operation of voluntary-defender systems. It is significant in this connection that there is recognition of the need and a desire on the part of the voluntary-defender organizations studied to serve in all of the criminal courts in their communities.

The scope of representation afforded by a voluntary-defender system may also be limited by the opposition of the Bar or of the Bench. The resistance of segments of the Bar[17] to a voluntary-defender system has been reflected in the attitude of the Bench in some places. In certain cases, this pressure has been so great that the judiciary has continued to assign individual attorneys even though the services of a voluntary-defender system were available.

Finally, the scope of representation which a voluntary-defender system can afford may be limited by the physical arrangements of the courts. This is the case, to some extent, in Philadelphia. There the lower courts with limited original criminal jurisdiction, the Magistrates' Courts, are so dispersed throughout the city that the Philadelphia Voluntary Defender Association does not have the manpower to extend its coverage to those courts. This committee understands that, if these courts were centralized in location, the Philadelphia Voluntary Defender Association could appear in them without a substantial increase in its present staff and would seek to extend its services to them.

Where the needed funds are available and the value of the organization has been recognized, experience has shown that it is not difficult for a voluntary-defender system to extend its services to courts other than those which it originally served. The fact that a voluntary-defender system can expand when the conditions are favorable is shown by the recent growth of the Criminal Courts Branch of the Legal Aid Society of New York. At the end of 1948, the Criminal Courts Branch was providing service to indigent accused in the Felony Part and Youth Term of the Magistrates' Court for the Borough of Manhattan and the courts of Special

Sessions and General Sessions for New York County. In addition, it represented indigent youths in the Youth Term of Magistrates' Court for the Borough of the Bronx. By the end of 1956, the services of the Criminal Courts Branch had been extended to include the Federal District Courts of the Eastern and Southern Districts of New York, the Women's Court of the Magistrates' Court for the Borough of Manhattan, two other courts in Bronx County and two courts in Kings County.[18]

This growth was spurred by general recognition of the high quality of the representation which the society gives to its indigent clients. Judges of courts which were not covered in 1948 requested that the Criminal Courts Branch extend its operation to their courts.[19] Thus, in New York City, the presence of an effective voluntary-defender system in a few courts was a powerful impetus, in itself, for expansion.

2. The Quality of Representation

(a) *The Voluntary-Defender System Can Provide Representation Which Is Experienced, Competent, and Zealous.*

Voluntary-defender systems are, in the judgment of this committee, able to afford experienced, competent, and zealous representation. Since voluntary-defender systems are built on the "law office" principle, a continuity of qualified representation is possible. The young lawyer may be trained before he undertakes the more difficult responsibilities of defense and a pool of knowledge and experience can be created which is not available to the casually assigned defense attorney. In all of the jurisdictions which were studied, the voluntary-defender systems had the reputation of giving representation of a quality equal to that given by the more qualified private attorneys who appear in the criminal courts.

(b) *The Voluntary-Defender System Can Provide the Investigatory and Other Facilities Necessary for a Complete Defense.*

If given sufficient funds, the voluntary-defender system can provide the investigatory and other facilities necessary for a complete defense. However, all voluntary-defender systems studied by this committee have expressed a need for more funds for facilities for investigation. This need is particularly acute where the voluntary-defender office is composed of a single attorney. In such a case, the voluntary defender must necessarily spend much of his time in court and cannot devote himself to investigation. There is no reason, however, why any voluntary-defender system, if provided with sufficient funds, cannot establish the required facilities for investigation.

> (c)   *The Voluntary-Defender System Can Come Into Operation at a Sufficiently Early Stage of the Proceedings So That It Can Fully Advise and Protect and Can Also Continue Through Appeal.*

Since a voluntary-defender system is an organization in being, it is in a position to initiate its representation as early as advisable. The various voluntary-defender systems studied by this committee have tried to shorten the time between arrest and their first contact with the defendant. In New York County, the Criminal Courts Branch of the Legal Aid Society generally begins its representation within 48 to 72 hours after arrest.

This would be true, as well, of the Philadelphia Voluntary Defender Association were it not for the fact that the office does not have the staff to service the many magistrates' courts spread throughout the city. Consequently, the Philadelphia association initiates its representation after a defendant has been sent to the county prison to await the action of the county court.[20] The Criminal Branch of the New Orleans Legal Aid Society must also defer its representation until a prisoner is in the parish prison awaiting action by the District Court. Its staff is not large enough to represent indigents at any earlier time.[21]

> (d)   *The Voluntary-Defender System Provides for Undivided Loyalty by Defense Counsel to the Indigent Defendant.*

There is no reason why a voluntary-defender system should not provide representation that is completely loyal to the client. Nor has this committee observed any situations in which the interests of the client have not been fully served. It concludes that a voluntary-defender system can, and that the presently existing voluntary-defender systems do, meet this standard.

3.   The Community's Responsibility

A voluntary-defender system is a focal point upon which community interest may center. The board of directors of the voluntary-defender offices studied by this committee generally have been composed by leaders of the Bar and the community generally. In this manner, the community has had the opportunity to take an active role in providing representation for the indigent in the criminal courts and through such participation it has become aware of the need for such representation. A voluntary-defender system can also by its own activity generate public interest in and increase public concern with the problem of representing the indigent. Thus, it performs the dual function of providing an institution through which the community's responsibility can be discharged and an instrument which can increase the community's awareness of its responsibility.

The funds which a voluntary-defender system receives from the community are, in some measure at least, an index of the extent to which the community is willing to discharge its responsibility toward indigent defendants. If the relationship between the voluntary-defender system and the community is a cordial one, it can be a source of great strength for the system. One of the reasons for the signal success of the Criminal Courts Branch of the New York Legal Aid Society is the interest which the community has shown in its activities. This interest is reflected not only in the substantial charitable contributions made to the society by the general public but also by the fact that distinguished members of the public, as well as the Bar, serve on the society's Board of Directors.[22]

C. *The Public-Defender System*

1. The Scope of Representation

The scope of representation which a public-defender system can provide is established by the statute which creates the system and by the funds which the state is willing to appropriate to support the system. There is no inherent limitation upon the scope of representation which a public defender system can provide in the courts of its jurisdiction and some public defender systems function in all criminal courts.[23] Many, however, do not appear in lower courts to represent indigents charged with minor crimes.

The fact that public-defender systems are created by statute, however, makes it particularly important that provision for improvement and expansion be made at the outset. If this is not done, it may be difficult to secure the required statutory amendments to extend the scope of the public-defender system. An example of this problem is provided by the public-defender system as it operates in Cook County, Illinois. The act establishing public defenders in Illinois empowers them to act before "any court of record exercising general criminal jurisdiction" within the county.[24] This restrictive statutory language has prevented the public defender from entering the lower city courts with limited jurisdiction.

2. The Quality of Representation

(a) *The Public-Defender System Can Provide Representation Which Is Experienced, Competent, and Zealous.*

As in the case of the voluntary-defender system, the "law office" approach of a public-defender organization allows experienced, competent, and zealous representation to be afforded the indigent accused. It is clear that there is nothing inherent in a properly constituted public-defender system which prevents its providing such representation.

In most of the jurisdictions examined by this committee, the public-defender system has the reputation of giving representation of a quality equal to that of the more qualified private attorneys who practice in the criminal courts. In general, the standard of representation established by this committee has been met by the public-defender system. This conclusion is confirmed by a recent study of the system which found:

Public Defender Offices originated in the need for representation of the indigent criminal defendant. They have survived because they appear to be performing the task allotted them in a satisfactory manner.[25]

(b) *The Public-Defender System Is Capable of Providing the Investigatory and Other Facilities Necessary for a Complete Defense.*

If sufficient funds are available, the public defender, like the voluntary defender, may provide the investigatory and other facilities necessary for a complete defense. Thus, for example, the Public Defender Office of Alameda County, California, has a revolving fund of $1,000, an amount generous enough to permit travel at a moment's notice to any point in the United States.[26] On the other hand, however, the surveys conducted by this committee indicate that most public-defender offices are seeking additional investigatory facilities. In Marin County, California, the public defender has no investigator, and relies extensively upon information furnished by the prosecutor's office. In Connecticut it is necessary for the public defenders to secure the approval, on a case-by-case basis, of the Chief Justice of the Supreme Court of Errors before incurring expenses for personnel to conduct factual investigations.[27] The practical difficulties and inconveniences of this procedure are such that, at the risk of having to take the witness stand and not being able to continue as defense counsel, the Hartford County public defender conducts his own investigation and also relies heavily upon the prosecution for necessary information and in Fairfield County, the public defender depends largely upon his own ability to find and interview the necessary witnesses. The public defender in New Haven uses law students from the Law School of Yale University.[28]

This committee concludes that nothing within the public-defender approach precludes its developing sufficient means to secure necessary information. The fault, where it exists, lies not in the method, but in the supervisory unit's inability or unwillingness to provide the appropriations necessary for improved services.

(c) *The Public-Defender System Can Come into Operation at a Sufficiently Early Stage of the Proceedings So That It Can Fully Advise and Protect and Can also Continue Through Appeal.*

The public defender, like the voluntary defender, generally functions through an operating "law office." As such, in the absence of statutory limitations, he may initiate his services as early as desirable, and may also continue to provide representation through the appellate process. In Alameda County, California, for example, the public defender generally interviews an indigent defendant within forty-eight hours after arrest. This public defender also prosecutes an appeal whenever, in his opinion, the available grounds for appeal are meritorious.[29]

(d) *The Public-Defender System Is Capable of Providing for Undivided Loyalty by Defense Counsel to the Indigent Accused.*

This committee concludes that there is no reason why a public-defender system, properly constituted and with proper safeguards, cannot assure undivided loyalty by defense counsel to the indigent accused. The committee is mindful, however, of the objection that is sometimes voiced that the loyalty and independence of counsel may be affected where the state assumes all phases of prosecution and defense.[30]

The committee recognizes that, in a community dominated by a powerful and corrupt political organization which either directly or indirectly controls all appointments and nominations to public office, a public-defender system, as any other governmental agency, may not serve the purpose for which it was created. In such a community, the charge that an indigent defendant was being prosecuted and defended by the same political authority would have a practical, as well as a theoretical, reality. The surveys conducted by this committee have indicated, on the one hand, that this danger may not be entirely imaginary, but that, on the other hand, public defenders in general are completely loyal to their clients. It should be emphasized, however, that the mere fact that the defense of indigents is formalized within the control of an attorney retained by the government does not, by itself, mean that the attorney will not operate with complete loyalty and devotion to the interests of his client.

Whether a public-defender system is desirable in a given community must be judged by the community itself in the light, first, of the political climate of the community and, second, of the practicability of setting up the system in such a manner that it not only will be in fact, but will be generally recognized as being, entirely free from political influence or control. This committee believes that there are certain safeguards which will tend to minimize or prevent the danger of such influence or control. These will be discussed in Chapter VI.

3. The Community's Responsibility

In a certain sense, the public-defender system is a true reflection of the community's responsibility for the defense of the indigent. The existence of a public-defender system indicates that the community has been sufficiently concerned with the problem of the indigent defendant to establish a public office and to appropriate public funds.

The ease with which the community can partially discharge its responsibility through the public defender creates, in itself, another danger: the community may believe that the mere establishment of a public defender system is a sufficient discharge of its responsibility. This is not true and the effectiveness of any public defender will be impeded if the public believes that it has entirely fulfilled its obligation by establishing the system. With the passage of time, the statutory scheme may become ineffective unless the public continues to be concerned with and to support the system.

D. *The Mixed Private-Public System*

This system has been in operation for only a comparatively short period of time and in a limited number of jurisdictions. Essentially, however, it is close to the voluntary-defender operation in theory and in practice. The mixed private-public system, in the judgment of this committee, has great potentialities and should be seriously considered by communities which are either re-examining an existing defender system or seeking to establish a new defender system.

The principal inherent advantage of the mixed private-public system is, in the opinion of this committee, that it can draw upon public funds (as well as private contributions) and thereby finance wide coverage and competent defense while, at the same time, it eliminates any question of political control or domination. Moreover, the merger of the interests of the community, the legal profession, and government, as exemplified by the Buffalo, Rochester, and Puerto Rican approach, focuses the attention and unites the efforts of all those who should be concerned with the problem of representation of indigent defendants. The committee believes that this dynamic system should be able in practice to realize its full potential and meet all of the standards essential for adequate representation enumerated in this report.

Note to Chapter V

The Assigned-Counsel System and Capital Cases

Since the main concern of this study has been the defense of indigents in non-capital cases, the committee has not made an independent examination of the assignment of counsel in capital cases. The committee considered such assignments when they were an integral part of the systems which were surveyed. The Appendix will indicate the number of states providing compensation, expenses, or both to counsel so assigned.

Generally, cases involving the death penalty have evoked a deep concern on the part of the judiciary. Prior to the decision of the Supreme Court in *Powell* v. *Alabama*, 287 U. S. 45 (1932), there were many assignments to indigent defendants charged with a capital offense.[31] This fact is noted by Professor Beaney who states:

> *The lack of cases in which the petitioner claimed a failure to appoint counsel or to appoint effective counsel in the years immediately following the Powell case suggests that states were for the most part careful in capital cases.*[32]

On the basis of its study, this committee is impressed by two factors in connection with the assignment of counsel to represent indigent defendants charged with a capital crime.

(a) *Cost of Assigned Counsel.*

The surveys conducted by the staff of this committee show that, in some of the communities where assigned counsel are compensated and/or reimbursed and where there is a central defender system in the same community, the cost of such representation is roughly equivalent to the sums necessary to maintain the central defender office. The following comparisons illustrate this point:

COMPARISON OF COSTS BETWEEN
DEFENDER ORGANIZATIONS AND PAYMENTS
TO ASSIGNED COUNSEL[33]

	COSTS OF DEFENDER ORGANIZATION	PAYMENT TO ASSIGNED COUNSEL FOR CAPITAL CASES
Philadelphia Voluntary Defender Association	$65,566.27*	$61,516.41**
Dade County Florida, Public Defender: 1956–57***	16,300.00	20,000.00

*   *June 1, 1956–May 31, 1957.*
**   *1957 Calendar Year.*
*** *October 1, 1956–July 30, 1957. Note that the County Budget for this year indicated an additional expenditure of $5,000.00 for the court stenographer in insolvency cases. County Budget of Dade County, Florida, 1956–1957, p. 20.*

(b)   *Time of Representation.*

The surveys conducted by the staff of this committee also show that, in a few communities in which the compensated and/or reimbursed assigned-counsel system exists jointly with a central defender office, counsel may not be assigned in capital cases until the defendant has been indicted (see Appendix), whereas the central defender office may initiate its representation in non-capital cases prior to the filing of an indictment or information against the accused. An excellent example is to be found in Philadelphia where the Voluntary Defender Association does not represent indigents charged with capital crimes. The association initiates representation, upon request, after the defendant has been incarcerated in the county jail. In the great majority of cases, this is before indictment. On the other hand, counsel are assigned to represent indigents charged with capital offenses upon arraignment in the county court in Philadelphia.

Chapter VI

Recommendations

This report begins by quoting the remark of the Chief Justice of the United States that "One of the characteristics that has ennobled this nation and made it great is our insistence upon making justice equal and accessible for all." It is with deep concern that this committee must state that the fundamental conclusion which it has reached is that, in many places in the United States today, justice is not "equal and accessible for all." With the exception of a few jurisdictions, not all indigent defendants are adequately represented. The committee cannot emphasize too strongly its basic recommendation that each community study the problem of the indigent defendant as it exists for it and take, as soon as possible, whatever action is required to provide adequate representation to all accused, irrespective of their financial means.

Although the committee is impressed by the tremendous task which lies ahead, it is encouraged in the hope that this task may be successfully and speedily accomplished by the rapid strides which defender systems and legal aid offices have taken in the last few decades. This growth is encouraging not only because it shows what can be done by interested communities and dedicated individuals but also because it makes it possible to re-evaluate existing approaches so that future growth may profit from the experience of the past.[1] The experience of other communities will be, this committee believes, of invaluable help in establishing or improving a local defender system. Not only will mistakes be avoided in administrative and operating policies but greater efficiency may be achieved. There is also an advantage in adopting tested procedures and standardized forms and reports so as to make possible valid comparison with systems in other jurisdictions.

The Standing Committee on Legal Aid Work of the American Bar Association and the National Legal Aid and Defender Association stand ready to assist state and local Bar associations and organizing committees with pamphlets, studies and other materials.[2] They may also be able to provide the technical help of an expert to consult with the local group. It is suggested that the facilities of these national organizations be made use of whenever a community is seeking to establish a new defender system or is reviewing its existing defender system.

The specific recommendations which this committee has formulated fall into three categories. The first deals with recommendations of general application which are intended to aid a community in selecting the type of system most suitable to its character and its needs. The second category comprises recommendations which apply to all defender systems and are useful in that they should make it possible for any system to function more efficiently. The third is composed of those recommendations which make specific suggestions as to how each type of defender system might be improved.

A. Recommendations Relating to the Choice of a System

It is important to determine at the outset whether conditions which exist in a community create problems which can be dealt with more effectively by one type of defender system than by another. When a community considers the type of defender system it should adopt, at least four factors should be examined, each of which may have a decided effect upon the choice of system and its procedures when established. These are:

1. The type and size of the community;

2. The number of indigent accused;

3. The probable cost to the community and its capacity to meet this cost; and

4. Conditions within the local Bar.

1. The Type and Size of the Community

The committee has concluded that in rural communities any one of the recognized defender systems may be successfully employed. In sizable urban communities, however, it was the committee's conclusion that the typical assigned-counsel system does not function well. Moreover, the survey of Tompkins County, New York, casts serious doubts on the effectiveness of the typical assigned-counsel system even in urban centers of a moderate size. Therefore, any urban community with a population greater than 30,000 to 40,000 should, in the opinion of this committee, give serious consideration to another type of system.

2. The Number of Indigent Accused

Another essential consideration at the outset is a determination of the number of indigent defendants within the community: how many of the criminally accused are unable to afford counsel?

There have been various general estimates as to the number of indigents appearing in the criminal courts requiring the appointment of counsel. Emery A. Brownell, the author of *Legal Aid in the United States*, has estimated that 60 per cent of the defendants in the criminal courts are without funds to employ counsel.[3] The surveys conducted by the staff of this committee indicate that the percentage generally runs somewhat lower, varying from jurisdiction to jurisdiction and ranging from approximately 30 to 60 per cent.[4] It should be noted, however, that the statistics compiled by the staff did not at all times take into account proceedings such as probation hearings and writs of habeas corpus. Hence, the percentages derived from the staff's surveys might be somewhat increased to bring them closer to actuality.

The important point, however, is that the number of indigent accused requiring assistance of counsel is large in most jurisdictions and that it varies from community to community, and even from court to court within each community. Each community should, when it begins consideration of the appropriate defender system for its needs, estimate roughly the number of indigent criminal defendants which its system may have to serve. The yardsticks suggested above, coupled with the experience of judges, prosecutors, and defense counsel, should permit a reasonably accurate estimate. If the number of indigent defendants is relatively large in relation to the total number of defendants in the criminal courts, the community should seriously consider whether its needs can be effectively served by the typical assigned-counsel system.

3. The Probable Cost to the Community and Its Capacity to Meet This Cost

All communities should recognize that the lack of effective representation itself creates a social cost. In the long run, no community can afford to provide one standard of justice for the rich and another for the poor. If a community elects to provide representation only in situations where representation is required by the Constitution of the United States and if it selects the typical assigned-counsel system, it has not necessarily escaped, by avoiding a direct financial outlay, a potential social cost of considerable magnitude. If the typical assigned-counsel system is not adequate to meet the need for representation, the basic problem remains unsolved. Finally, it should be noted that a system that works efficiently may save a community more than its cost by eliminating some delays in the administration of criminal justice, thus reducing local detention costs and decreasing the burden on the judiciary and the prosecution.

If a community is considering an assigned-counsel system in which an adequate fee will be paid for each assignment, it should review the experience of other communities as to the cost of this solution. The experience has generally been that this system is more expensive than the establishment of a voluntary- or public-defender system. For example, in Marin County, California, the total of fees paid to assigned counsel in capital cases was so high as to be an important factor in the establishment of a public-defender system.[5] The experience of Baltimore, Philadelphia, and Dade County, Florida with the payment of fees to assigned counsel in capital cases also indicates that the total expense of an assigned-counsel system in which adequate fees are paid is likely to be very large.[6]

On the other hand, if a community is considering the voluntary-defender system or the public-defender system, there will be direct expenses which must be met, in the former system by charitable contributions and in the latter by public appropriations. This committee has concluded that in order to provide coverage which it considers adequate, the budget of a voluntary- or public-defender system should range from 15 to 25 per cent of that of the public prosecutor.[7]

If it seems unlikely that the required financial support can be attained through charitable contributions, a community may give particular attention to the establishment of a public-defender system. Or it might also consider solving the financial problem by adopting a mixed private-public system similar to that used in

Rochester and Buffalo.[8] In many states the adoption of the mixed private-public system will require the passage of enabling legislation. Consideration should also be given to any possible difficulty created by limitations in the state's constitution with respect to the granting of funds to private organizations.[9]

4. Conditions Within the Local Bar

Conditions within the local Bar vary widely in the United States. In most metropolitan centers the Bar must be equipped to handle legal problems arising from large scale corporate activity[10] as well as the problems typical of the family and small business. This has resulted in the growth in many cities of law firms of great size. Lawyers have tended to specialize and many have developed a type of practice in which they never enter the courtroom either for the purpose of civil or criminal litigation.

Where a specialized bar exists, it is unlikely that the assigned-counsel system will operate well. It will fail to operate well not because the Bar is unwilling to cooperate but because the lack of familiarity of a large proportion of the Bar with trial practice, and in particular with criminal matters, vitiates one of the fundamental assumptions of the assigned-counsel system: that each member of the Bar is capable of giving adequate representation when assigned to defend an indigent criminal defendant.

The specialized Bar is less prevalent in the smaller rural communities of the United States. In a rural community of, for example, 10,000 inhabitants, the lawyer, like the doctor, is usually a general practitioner. His practice relates to all of the legal problems which his community generates: family problems such as divorce, wills and estates and conveyances; corporate problems; and civil and criminal litigation.

The attitude of the local Bar towards the defense of indigents is, of course, a factor to be considered in all defender systems. The assigned-counsel system can never function well unless supported by the local Bar. The voluntary- and public-defender systems will always function better where the Bar understands the defender function and co-operates with the defender organization toward the end that all persons in the community charged with crime who need the assistance of counsel are represented by counsel.

B. *Recommendations Relating to the Organization and More Efficient Functioning of All Systems*

This committee believes that the operation of any type of defender system may be improved (1) by the use of an advisory board, (2) by the use of a panel of practicing lawyers to determine indigency where indigency is in question, and (3) by the requirement of an annual report which can serve to keep the public informed and solicit its support. Those communities which have established systems which do not incorporate these features might well consider their usefulness in improving the operations of their present systems and, where a community is establishing a new system, it should consider the advisability of designing its system in such a way that advantage can be taken of these techniques. Of course, the greatest potential for improvement and usefulness lies in the adoption of all three of these suggestions. However, they are not interdependent and there is nothing which should prevent the adoption of some rather than all of them.

1. The Advisory Board

An advisory board can perform many functions. If drawn from a cross section of the Bar and the public, such a board provides a connecting link between the system and the general public. This permits the system to keep in close touch with the trends of public opinion and also provides a technique through which the problems and needs of the system can be conveyed to the public. Boards of this type can also perform a critically important function in shielding the defender system from public[11] and judicial pressures. When the system is called upon to represent an "unpopular" defendant, the board can explain to the public, in a way in which the personnel of the system could not, the reasons why this defendant must be afforded the same representation as other defendants. Furthermore, the fact that the defender system has the backing of a representative and distinguished advisory board will make it easier to resist pressures from the judiciary. Such pressures are not common. Usually they arise from well-meaning efforts of individual judges. It may, however, be difficult for the defender, who appears almost daily in court, to remain completely unaffected by them. Finally, the advisory board creates an opportunity for a defender system to present its problems to a sympathetic audience in search of guidance and support. This may be of particular importance in relation to the long-run development of the system because it affords an opportunity for careful weighing of any programs before they are initiated and permits the wide experience of the supervisory board to be brought to bear upon the problems of the system.

The technique of the advisory board so far has been applied

only to the voluntary-defender system. Florence M. Kelley, Attorney-in-Charge of the Criminal Courts Branch of the New York Legal Aid Society, has characterized the importance of the board of directors of that society as follows:

The greatest strength of the New York Legal Aid Society is its Board of Directors and its officers. This Board is composed mainly of lawyers, most of whom are extremely active as practitioners and as members of organized bar associations; they are outstanding members of the legal profession in New York City. There are other directors who represent the community as a whole. The Board of Directors selects the staff of the Society and this staff is responsible only to the Board. The Board gives generously of its time to the problems of the Society, both as to administration and principle. It is at once founder and guide. The staff member is encouraged to accept responsibility within the framework of operation determined upon by the Board. To the staff, the Board is a tower of strength. If the ideal defender office is approached in any measure by the operations of the New York Legal Aid Society Criminal Courts Branch, it is and will be because the Board will accept no less.[12]

The need for an advisory board has been recognized in a few areas in which the public defender system operates. In Chicago, Illinois, for example, an attempt is being made to establish an advisory board. Mr. George Nye, the public defender of Alameda County, has stated in this regard that the public defender suffers from

. . . the absence of a formal link with the community, such as is provided by the directors or advisory board of a conventional legal aid agency. This lack derives from an effort to establish the public defender in as independent a situation as possible. But as a result he has been isolated from the community in all important respects save one—his umbilical dependence upon local authorities for seasonal apppropriations. Conceivably the defender would be in a more effective position if the power of his appropriating and financing authority were shared by a group representative of community interests, and particularly those of the profession.[13]

Although this committee knows of no instance in which an advisory board has been established in connection with the operations of an assigned-counsel system, there is no insurmountable obstacle to the use of an advisory board for such systems. In particular, where the New Jersey system is in operation, it would seem relatively simple to establish a link between the system and the community by a supervisory board. Although the problem is more difficult where the typical assigned-counsel system is used, a representative group of the community could be constituted to observe the operation of the system and to consult with the judiciary and the bar association on the problems faced by the system and the way in which those problems might be met.

2. The Reference Panel

One of the difficult questions faced by any defender system is that of deciding whether to represent a defendant whose claim to eligibility is doubtful. This problem is of particular significance in connection with the relation of the system to the Bar. An eminently practical solution has been evolved by the public defender of Alameda County, California. The Bar association in that community has a list of attorneys who have expressed an interest in representing defendants whose eligibility is in doubt. When the public defender has a case in which indigency is questionable, he refers the matters to three attorneys, selected by the Bar association from its Bar reference service panel. Each of these attorneys interviews the defendant and any one of them may decide to represent him. If all three decide that the defendant is without funds, the matter will be returned to the public defender.

This device not only provides a helpful technique for determining borderline cases of indigency but also obviates the complaint that the defender system is depriving the Bar of fees by making it possible for practicing attorneys to undertake representations where there is a prospect of a minimal fee. Moreover, such a panel might also be used to provide representation for indigent defendants who cannot be represented by the defender organization because of a conflict of interests.

There is nothing inherent in the structure or operations of the voluntary-defender system or the assigned-counsel system which would prevent the application of the same technique to them. The nature of the problem faced by the voluntary-defender system is precisely the same as that faced by the public-defender system. The lack of centralization which is typical of assigned-counsel systems makes it somewhat more difficult to apply this technique to them but, if the judiciary will cooperate, the panel principle could be effectively applied within the framework of the assigned-counsel system. Moreover, it should be noted that this principle could be very easily applied to the assigned-counsel system by the adoption of this committee's recommendation that the actual assignment of attorneys to represent indigent defendants be placed in the hands of a single administrative unit of the courts. This recommendation is discussed later in this report.[14]

3. The Annual Report

The annual report is rather extensively employed by voluntary- and public-defender systems. It can also be used by the New Jersey type of assigned-counsel system. The lack of centralization of the typical assigned-counsel system makes annual reporting more difficult but some report could be incorporated in any annual report of the judicial system.

The annual report of a defender system can serve many functions. It can be a repository of the system's history and can contain periodic statements of its aspirations. It furnishes an occasion for a thoughtful yearly analysis of the work of the system and an opportunity to report to the public on the problems and progress of the system. As such, it can be a useful bridge between the system and the community and can foster community understanding and support. Finally, it can supply information and statistics which will be useful in comparing the cost and effectiveness of the community's system with those of other communities.

This committee believes that each defender system should issue annual reports acquainting the public with changes in personnel, cases handled and their disposition, prospective changes in policy and procedure, and financial and other information of public concern. Local community conditions and the resources of the defender system must determine how much further than annual reporting each defender system should go in disseminating information about its activities, needs and accomplishments. An expanded public information program might include, for example, a quarterly such as *The Legal Aid Review*, published by the New York Legal Aid Society. This review offers readable articles, often written by experts in the field, ranging beyond the particular system's needs and activities and into descriptions of other systems and the philosophy underlying defender systems.

C. *Specific Recommendations Relating to Individual Systems*

The last category of recommendations by this committee is composed of specific suggestions for the improvement of the various types of defender systems. They are not meant to be exclusive but are merely intended to suggest some specific techniques which might be used to improve the performance of the system.

1. The Assigned-Counsel System

This committee believes that the typical assigned-counsel system may be improved by:

1. Using rotation to assign *qualified* counsel;

2. Centralizing assignment in a single administrative unit;

3. Having indigency determined by someone other than the assigned counsel;

4. Providing for the reimbursement of assigned counsel for all expenses incurred; and

5. Compensating counsel adequately.

(a) Assignments Should Be Made by Rotation

This committee believes that the New Jersey system of assigned counsel represents a significant advance and improvement over the typical system. The principle of rotation, on which the New Jersey system is based, is designed to enlist all attorneys in the effort to provide adequate representation. It is fairer to the Bar as a whole than the typical assigned-counsel system which generally imposes heavy burdens on a few and little, if any, burden on most members of the Bar. The principle of rotation is also desirable because it should expand the interest of the Bar in the criminal law and the administration of criminal justice.

However, the principle of rotation has within it a latent difficulty in that it assumes that each member of the Bar is capable of acting in any criminal case to which he is assigned. Therefore, in many communities it would be undesirable to apply the principle of rotation without making some provision to correct this defect. This problem might be met, in the opinion of this committee, by a system of rotation in which an inexperienced attorney is assigned with an experienced attorney. Such an approach will initially, of course, increase the frequency of appointments. However, it will permit the rapid growth of the experience of the members of the Bar with criminal law which, in turn, should in the long run permit a return to a system of single assignment, except for dual assignments in the case of attorneys recently admitted to the Bar. Moreover, the assignment of an experienced attorney to each case will assure the indigent defendant of more capable representation than is generally possible under the usual rotation system.

(b) Assignments Should Be Made by a Single Administrative Unit

Every assigned-counsel system should consider the establishment of a single administrative unit to make all assignments of counsel.

This approach has a number of significant advantages. First, it permits assignments to be made before arraignment, thus assisting the assigned-counsel system in meeting the standard of timeliness which this committee views as so important in providing adequate representation.[15] Second, it may serve to insulate, at least to some extent, assigned counsel from outside pressures and thus assure more complete loyalty of counsel to the indigent defendant.[16]

Assignment by a single administrative unit also permits a more careful planning of assignments than is possible where assignments are made by the judge in the courtroom. The administrative unit is in a position to assign any member of the Bar, and is not limited to the one who is known to the judge, or who is next on the list under a rotation system. It permits the assignment of an inexperienced attorney with a more qualified member of the Bar and simplifies the administration of this committee's first recommendation for the improvement of the assigned-counsel system. Finally, such a technique would also facilitate the implementation of this committee's next two recommendations with respect to the assigned-counsel system.

(c) *Indigency Should Be Determined by Someone Other Than Assigned Counsel*

Assigned counsel should not determine whether the defendant to be represented is in fact indigent. This decision should be made, as far as possible, prior to assignment as part of the initial decision to assign counsel. If this is to be done, there must be some central organization charged with the duty of investigating cases where the indigency of the defendant is doubtful. A central administrative unit of the courts charged with assignment could perform this function well.

There are two basic reasons why the function of determining indigency should not be performed by assigned counsel. If assigned counsel reviews the indigency of his assigned client, he may consume a considerable amount of time and effort which should be spent in preparing to defend the case. In addition, if this determination is left to assigned counsel, the possibility of abuse is always present. Assigned counsel may attempt to secure compensation from the family or friends of the accused thereby applying a standard of indigency different from that used by the assigning body. Judge Edward J. Dimock has commented in describing the initial meeting between defendant and assigned counsel, at a time when the assigned-counsel system prevailed in the New York Court of General Sessions:

*The conference would ostensibly concern the facts of the case but,
in reality, was a searching inquiry, rather similar to an examination in proceedings supplementary to execution, designed to disclose
any assets possessed by the accused or his relatives or friends. . . .*[17]

(d) Assigned Counsel Should Be Reimbursed for Expenses

If assigned counsel are to have at their command the investigatory
and other facilities which this committee believes are essential for
adequate defense, it is imperative that they be reimbursed for any
expenses incurred in connection with investigations of fact, the
employment of expert witnesses, stenographic assistance, and the
other expenditures which are generally necessary to prepare for
and present a case in the criminal courts. Reimbursement of
assigned counsel for such expenses would provide the means for
assigned counsel to present an adequate defense and would also
remove the obvious inequity of requiring members of the Bar not
only to give their time but also to pay whatever expenses they
deem necessary in the defense of indigents.

This recommendation could be most easily implemented through
the use of a central administrative unit for assignments. This unit
could seek the budgetary appropriations required and would provide a central office through which claims for reimbursement
could be processed. In the long run, the investigatory and support-
ing functions for assigned counsel might be taken over completely
by this central administrative unit. It could undoubtedly furnish
investigatory facilities for all assignments at a lower cost than if
each individual counsel were reimbursed and might also be able to
furnish certain stenographic and other services at a lower cost
than if such services were provided on an individual basis.

(e) Assigned Counsel Should Be Compensated

There would seem to be little doubt that a higher quality of
representation can be achieved through the assigned-counsel system if assigned counsel are compensated. Care should be exercised
so that assignment does not develop into a patronage system. The
principal objection to compensation for assigned counsel is, of
course, the great expense involved where there are large numbers
of indigent defendants. However, in rural communities where the
number of indigent defendants is small, compensation might be a
feasible way of improving the general quality of representation
afforded by assigned counsel. Moreover, since such compensation

would usually be less than the assigned counsel would be paid by a private client, a desirable sharing of the economic burden between the Bar and the community would be achieved.

2. The Voluntary-Defender System

This committee believes that a voluntary-defender system may be improved by:

1. Seeking the support of the practicing Bar through voluntary service by members of the Bar and by making use of law students attending educational institutions in the community; and

2. Maintaining the quality of representation even if this can be done only by restricting coverage.

(a) *Voluntary Services of Members of the Bar and Law Students Should Be Sought*

The experience of the voluntary-defender systems of Boston, New York, and Philadelphia has indicated that individual attorneys are quite willing to assist the voluntary-defender office in representing indigent defendants. This assistance has taken several forms: large firms have sent associates to work with the voluntary defender for a specific period of time and individual attorneys have appeared to represent indigent defendants in particular cases and have undertaken the prosecution of appeals for the voluntary-defender office.

Many advantages accrue from this practice. The staff of the voluntary-defender office is supplemented at little or no expense; close and friendly relations between the practicing Bar and the voluntary-defender office are established and strengthened; and an opportunity is created for younger lawyers interested in trial work to become acquainted with trial practice and criminal law.[18] This development of an informed section of the practicing Bar should be helpful not only to the voluntary-defender system in the community but should also be beneficial to the entire administration of criminal justice.

Similar advantages are to be derived from a close relationship between a voluntary-defender office and a law school. A good example of such a relation is that between the Voluntary Defenders Committee, Inc. of Boston and the Harvard Law School. Those students of the Harvard Law School who are interested in legal aid in criminal cases perform useful services for the Voluntary

Defenders Committee and, again, young men are given an opportunity to learn something of the criminal law and the problems of defending the indigent.[19]

(b) *Quality Should Be Maintained*

One of the dilemmas which often faces a voluntary-defender system is whether coverage should be extended so that all indigents appearing in the criminal courts are afforded counsel or whether coverage should be restricted so that the quality of representation can be maintained. This committee hopes that, either through charitable contributions or through a combination of such contributions and public funds,[20] voluntary defenders will not be placed in a position where they must resolve this dilemma. However, if a choice is necessary, this committee believes that the quality of representation should be maintained even if as a consequence the coverage of the voluntary-defender system must be restricted.

This is, in the view of this committee, an important way in which conditions can be created which may lead to increased community support and expanded coverage by the voluntary-defender system. By demonstrating to the community what can be done through the voluntary-defender system, a strong inducement for an expansion of the system's coverage may be created. On the other hand, if the voluntary-defender system attempts to spread its facilities too thin, it may not be able to afford adequate representation, and this may in turn lead to dissatisfaction with the system and efforts to have it replaced by another.

3. The Public-Defender System

This committee believes that its recommendations concerning the voluntary-defender system apply equally to the public-defender system. It also has three specific recommendations with respect to public-defender systems. They may be improved by:

1. Securing enabling legislation which does not restrict the defender to service in particular courts, but permits expansion of the service as may be needed;

2. Appointing the public defender in such manner as to eliminate or minimize political influences and other influences which might affect his professional independence and his loyalty to his client; and

3. Providing an annual budget for the public defender system so as to avoid case-by-case requests for funds.

(a) *The Enabling Legislation Should Not Be Restrictive*

This committee recognizes that it may be impossible to secure the coverage which it believes desirable at the time when a public-defender system is initiated. If a public-defender system is established by a statute which restricts it to representation of indigent defendants in particular courts, it may be especially difficult to secure amendment to the statute when the public-defender system is in a position to expand its coverage. Therefore, the committee believes that it is particularly important that statutes creating public-defender systems should not contain limitations which might inhibit the future growth of the system.[21]

(b) *The Public Defender Should Be Appointed and Given Tenure in Such a Manner as to Eliminate or Minimize Political and Other Influences Which Might Affect His Professional Independence and His Loyalty to His Client*

The selection of the public defender and his staff is one of the essential considerations in the proper functioning of the public-defender system. As indicated in Chapter V of this report,[22] one of the objections often made to the public-defender system is that it does not provide for complete loyalty by defense counsel to the indigent accused. The committee does not believe that this defect is inherent in the public-defender system.

In the opinion of this committee, the selection system of Alameda County, California—civil service examination—works well. The committee's study has indicated, however, that there is some risk that the public defender's independence of action may be affected if he is appointed by the trial court before whom he practices. The committee is also of the opinion that a risk of improper political influence exists where the defender is elected or appointed periodically, whether directly or indirectly, by an elected official or any official subject to political control.

The precise means of selecting a public defender will vary from community to community. The important objective is, in the opinion of this committee, to establish a technique of appointment which operates so that the public defender is not subject to political and other outside influences which may inhibit his freedom of action. The public defender is effectively protected from such influences if he has tenure and if he is selected by a body other than the trial court such as, for example, an appellate court, or through a civil service examination[23] and, in turn, is given complete freedom to select his own assistants. An advisory board may also be effective in securing this end.

(c) The Public-Defender System Should Have an Annual Budget

This committee's surveys have convinced it that public-defender systems operate more effectively when they are given the freedom of an annual budget rather than being forced to secure all or part of the funds to be used in the defense of each case through separate appropriations. Thus, it is the considered judgment of the committee that the practice in Connecticut in which separate applications must be made for investigatory funds for each case in which such funds are to be used is not only cumbersome administratively but also tends to limit the investigation which the public defender can undertake.

If a public-defender system is to be afforded adequate facilities, it is undoubtedly cheaper for the community to provide the funds to support these facilities through a yearly appropriation rather than on a hand-to-mouth basis. The latter approach will inevitably reduce the effectiveness of public-defender systems by making investigations difficult and, in the long run, prove more expensive to the community. A public-defender system which can establish its own investigatory facilities should be able to do the necessary investigation at far less cost than a public-defender system which must meet its needs for investigation on an *ad hoc* basis.

4. The Mixed Private-Public System

In general, the recommendations which this committee has made with respect to voluntary-defender systems should apply to the mixed system.

This committee does not believe that the mixed system will generate any new or unusual problems. But that system does afford an unique opportunity by making it possible to support voluntary-defender systems wholly or partly by public funds. It is not required that support be received from both private and public sources; a defender system financed entirely by public funds but controlled by a private board of representative leaders of the Bar and community is a mixed system.

This committee is of the opinion that the mixed system deserves careful consideration as one of the best solutions to the problem of representing the indigent defendant. Where an existing voluntary-defender system is faced with financial difficulties or cannot expand its coverage because of lack of funds, the community might well consider supplementing voluntary contributions to the system by public funds.

Chapter VII

A Look Into the Future

In this report the committee has sought to examine objectively and without prejudice the various methods now in use for furnishing counsel to indigent accused. Each method appears to have its own points of strength and of weakness; each of them is capable of improvement. The committee has endeavored to expose both strengths and weaknesses and to recommend ways of improving existing systems.

The committee's aim has been to strengthen the traditional procedures in criminal cases which provide that equality before the law of which Americans are justly proud. No one proposes to weaken the prosecution of crime, or to help the guilty escape punishment. The committee is concerned, however, that, in the great urban and industrial growth which has overtaken the country, society keep effective those safeguards that give meaning to the "presumption of innocence." The committee has emphasized that, in our adversary system of determining truth, simple justice requires that the defendant as well as the state must be represented by counsel.

To assure that goal, many communities must establish new defender systems; others must reappraise their present systems. In each community the object must be to meet fully the local need. These defender systems must be adequate in scope and staff to meet the true need at the local level. Many of these community systems will be operated as public defenders supported by tax funds, others as privately supported defenders or as branches of legal aid societies, and still others as privately managed organizations supported in whole or in part by tax funds.

The form of organization, the committee has concluded, is important only insofar as it assists or impedes the attainment of the true objective, namely, to provide experienced counsel at the right time and in the places where they are needed; and to assure that the quality of professional service rendered is at least equal to that offered by the local Bar to those who can pay for legal representation. The committee has noted some of the considerations and influences that may detract from the integrity and efficiency of defender systems, both public and private, and has suggested ways and means of overcoming them.

As a practical matter, the success, failure, or mediocrity of a defender system is largely dependent upon the degree of interest and imagination that right-thinking local leaders bring to bear upon the problem as it exists in their community. The financial cost need only be a fraction of what is spent for prosecution and, as pointed out earlier, a good defender system tends to reduce the cost of administrating criminal justice. Moreover, it is not difficult to establish or maintain a defender system.

Lawyers, judges, and bar associations must of necessity play the leading part in establishing and guiding these community agencies. As Chief Justice Charles Evans Hughes put it:

Whatever else lawyers may accomplish in public affairs, it is their privilege and obligation to assure a competent administration of justice to the needy, so that no man shall suffer in the enforcement of his legal rights for want of a skilled protector, able, fearless and incorruptible.[1]

Lawyers and judges cannot be expected, however, to carry the full load. As this report emphasizes, the responsibility is a community responsibility. Just as the medical care of poor persons is shared by all citizens and is looked at as a community service, so also defender systems, if they are to be truly effective, should have the financial and moral support of the entire community.

The average citizen has a deep-rooted, almost instinctive sense of justice and is keenly aware that unequal justice is, as Chief Justice Warren has said, a contradiction in terms. He will do his share to support the necessary machinery, if the Bench and Bar will explain the need and show the way. Daniel Webster exaggerated but little when he said: "Justice, sir, is the great interest of man on earth."

The American promise of equal justice for all can become a reality in our land in a comparatively short time if the American people want it enough to make the relatively slight sacrifices required. There is no worthier cause.

Appendix

PROVISION FOR THE ASSIGNMENT OF COUNSEL FOR INDIGENT DEFENDANTS IN CRIMINAL CASES[1]

STATE	SITUATIONS IN WHICH ASSIGNABLE	WHEN ASSIGNED	WHOSE INSTANCE	COMPENSATION	CITATION
Alabama	a) capital offense	after indictment	mandatory	limit of two attorneys $50–$100	Ala. Code 1940, Title 15, §§318, 382
	b) automatic appeal (death sentence)	after appeal is entered	defendant's request[2]	max. $250	
Arizona	a) felony[3]	arraignment	mandatory	reasonable (at presiding court's discretion)	Ariz. Rev. Stat. Ann. 1956, §§13–161, 13–1673, 13–1721; Super. Ct. Crim. Rule 163
	b) appeals	no provision	no provision	reasonable (at Supreme Court's discretion)	
Arkansas	felonies	before arraignment	mandatory on request	limit of two attorneys; (permissive in counties with population under 100,000) $25–$250	Ark. Stat. Ann. 1947, §§43–1203, 43–2415

State					
California	a) all cases in which superior court has original jurisdiction and in which public defender does not represent defendant	preliminary examination[4]	mandatory on request	reasonable compensation as well as necessary expenses	Cal. Pen. Code, §§859, 859a, 987, 987a, 1239, 1240, 1241; Re Public Defender see Cal. Gov't. Code, §§27700-27711
	b) appeals in cases not represented by public defender[5]	no provision	no provision	reasonable fee	
Colorado	In district courts after defendants indicted or informed against for crimes or misdemeanors triable in district courts on indictment or information	no provision	discretion of court	fixed by court	Col. Rev. Stat. Ann. 1953, §§39-7-29-31
Connecticut	all crimes (public defender)[6]	at any stage	public defender	salary	Conn. Rev. Gen. Stat. 1949, §§8796, 3615
Delaware	a) capital offense or cases involving accomplice or accessory thereto	on trial	mandatory	judge's discretion after letter of notice from assigned attorney as to amount received "from any other source"	Del. Code Ann. 1953, §§11, 5103; Super. Ct. Crim. Rule 44

STATE	SITUATIONS IN WHICH ASSIGNABLE	WHEN ASSIGNED	WHOSE INSTANCE	COMPENSATION	CITATION
	b) any criminal prosecution	when "appears in court"	judge's discretion	same as above	
Florida	a) capital cases	no provision	mandatory	max. $500 for trial; max. $500 for appeal	Fla. Stat. Ann. 1955, §§909.21, 924.17, 924.23, 924.25(6); Laws of Fla. 1955, Ch. 30143
	b) appeals (death sentence)	no provision	mandatory	same as above	
	c) cases in all counties with pop. over 480,000 (public defender)[7]	on arraignment	mandatory	salary	
Georgia	a) capital felony	after indictment or on appeal (if no counsel has previously been appointed)	mandatory	trial: each att'y, $50–$150[8]; guilty plea: min. of $15; appeal: max. $250; both trial and appeal: expenses up to $500	Ga. Code Ann. 1947, §§27-3001-3003; Ga. Const. Art. I, §1, ¶75
	b) criminal offenses[9]	on trial	mandatory on request		
Idaho	a) all cases for arraignment	on arraignment	mandatory on request	reasonable	Idaho Code Ann. 1947, §§19-1512, 19-1513

	b) all cases for trial on information or indictment	on trial in district court	mandatory on request[10]	reasonable	Ill. Ann. Stats. 1957, Ch. 38, §§730, 730a; Ch. 110, §101.26; Ch. 34, §163C—]
Illinois	a) where person charged with crime[11]	no provision	mandatory	noncapital case: max. $150; capital case: max. of $15/day up to 5 days/prep. and $25/day for trial; max. of $250 per def. When writ of error from death sentence, max. of $1,000	
	b) crimes punishable by imprisonment in penitentiary	on arraignment	mandatory on request unless intelligently waived; defendant under 18 cannot plead guilty or waive indictment unless represented by counsel	same as above	
	c) cases of any criminal offense in courts of general criminal jurisdiction in all counties with pop. of 35,000 or more (public defender)[12]	no provision	mandatory	salary	

STATE	SITUATIONS IN WHICH ASSIGNABLE	WHEN ASSIGNED	WHOSE INSTANCE	COMPENSATION	CITATION
Indiana	all cases of persons accused of crime (public defender in counties with pop. between 110,000 and 175,000 and over 400,000. Also State public defender to represent those contesting their imprisonment after time for appeal has expired)	no provision	mandatory[13]	all but public defender at discretion of court[14]	Ind. Stat. Ann. 1933, §§9–3501 to 3503; §§4–2316 to 2318; §§13–1401 to 1406; Ind. Const., Art. I, §13
Iowa	all cases in which defendant arraigned[15]	on arraignment	mandatory on request	where hom. or offense punishable by life impris. $20/trial day. Other felonies—$10 in full. If atty. follows case into another county or appeals, compensation increased	Iowa Code Ann. 1946, §§775: 4–6

State	Cases	Timing	Mandatory/Discretionary	Compensation	Citation
Kansas	a) all cases of persons about to be arraigned on indictment or information b) appeal from death sentence	on arraignment after conviction	mandatory	max. $10/day	Kan. Gen. Stat. Ann. 1949, Ch. 62 §1304
Kentucky	a) misdemeanors when def. incarcerated and lower court not in session b) felonies[16]	no provision no provision	mandatory on request mandatory on request	expenses plus fee up to $300 none	Ky. Rev. Stat. Ann. 1955, §455.010; Crim. Code Pract. Title IV, §51; Ky. Const., §11
Louisiana	felonies[17]	no provision	mandatory on request	none	La. Rev. Stat. Ann. 1950, §§15:142, 15:143
Maine	a) cases punishable by life imprisonment b) other felonies	in superior court in superior court	mandatory discretionary on request of defendant[18]	reasonable discretion of court	Me. Rev. Stat. Ann. 1954, Ch. 148, §11
Maryland	cases in circuit courts and criminal court of Baltimore[19]	whenever necessary	discretion of court except where capital or "other serious" cases where mandatory unless waived	determined by appointing court	Md. Code Ann. 1957, Art. 26, §§11, 12; Rules of Proc., Rule 723(b)

STATE	SITUATIONS IN WHICH ASSIGNABLE	WHEN ASSIGNED	WHOSE INSTANCE	COMPENSATION	CITATION
Massachusetts[20]	capital cases	preliminary examination or arraignment	discretionary before arraignment, mandatory afterwards	reasonable compensation and expenses	Mass. Laws Ann. 1956, Ch. 276, §37A; Ch. 277, §§47, 55, 56; Ch. 263, §5
Michigan	any felony or misdemeanor	no provision[21]	discretion of court	reasonable. If attorney follows case into other county or appeals, compensation increased	Mich. Stat. Ann. 1954, §§28.854, 28.1253, 28.1254
Minnesota	felony and gross misdemeanors (public defender in Hennapin and Ramsey Counties)	arraignment	mandatory on request	max. $25 per day per counsel (up to two) for prep. and max. $50 per day in ct. plus reasonable exp. If post conviction proceeding, fee and exp. within discretion of Sup. Ct.[22]	Minn. Stat. Ann. 1945, §§611.07, 611.12, 611.13

State	Crimes covered	When appointed	Appointment	Compensation	Citation
Mississippi	capital crimes	when defendant in jail or indicted	mandatory[23]	(no more than two att'ys: compensation is per case) max: if guilty plea, $75; if trial, $150; if appeal, $250	Miss Code Ann. 1956, §2505
Missouri	felony cases[24]	before arraignment	mandatory on def. request. Waiver accepted unless charge and circumstances would result in injustice	no provision	Mo. Stat. Ann. 1953, §545.820; Sup. Ct. Rule 29.01
Montana	crimes in which defendant arraigned	before arraignment	mandatory on request	reasonable	Mont. Rev. Codes Ann. 1947, §§94-6512, 94-6513
Nebraska	capital crimes and those punishable by imprisonment in penitentiary. Public defender in counties with population over 200,000[25]	after indictment	mandatory	max. $300 except in homicide cases	Neb. Rev. Stat. 1943, §§29.1803-29-1805

STATE	SITUATIONS IN WHICH ASSIGNABLE	WHEN ASSIGNED	WHOSE INSTANCE	COMPENSATION	CITATION
Nevada	cases in which defendant arraigned and on appeal from justices' court to district court	on arraignment	mandatory on request	when appointed to defend person charged on indict. or info., up to $300. Added compensation if counsel appeals or follows case to another county	Laws of Nev. 1957, Ch. 36, p. 60 Nev. Rev. Stat. 1957, §§169.160, 174.120, 7.260
New Hampshire	a) capital crimes	after indictment	mandatory on request	max. $500 plus expenses	N. H. Rev. Stat. Ann. 1955, §§604, 604.2, 604.3, 605.1, 605.2
	b) crimes with possible punishment of three years	after being held for grand jury	mandatory on request	same as above	
	c) minors or those of unsound mind	before plea of guilty or trial	mandatory	reasonable	
New Jersey	all criminal cases	before arraignment "if possible"	mandatory on request	murder cases only: reasonable	N. J. Stat. Ann. 1951, Tit. 2A, §163-1; Sup. Ct. Rule 1:12-9

State	Offense	Time of appointment	Appointment	Compensation	Citation
New Mexico	crimes punishable by penitentiary sentence	no provision	mandatory	homicide: reasonable; other: min. $25, max. $100 (max. of 2 att'ys)	N. M. Stat. 1953, §§41-11-2, 41-11-3
New York	cases in which defendant arraigned	on arraignment	mandatory on request[26]	where charge is punishable by death or on appeal from judgment of death or life imprisonment, personal & incidental expenses plus up to $1500 (if one counsel) or $2000 (if more than one)	N. Y. Code of Cr. Proc., §§308, 308a, 8, 699; N. Y. Const., Art. I, §§6, 11
North Carolina	a) capital crimes	at any time	before def. bound over, discretionary; afterwards mandatory	court's discretion	N. C. Gen. Stat. 1955, §§15.4, 15.-4.1, 15.5
	b) all crimes	no provision	courts discretion[27]	no provision	
North Dakota	all criminal cases	no provision	mandatory on request	max. $25 per day in Dist. Ct., $50 per day in Co. Ct.	N. Dak. Rev. Code 1943, §§27-0831, 29-0127
Ohio	felony cases[28]	after indictment	mandatory	felony: up to $100; manslaughter: up to $350; murder: as court approves	Ohio Rev. Code Ann. 1953, §§2941.50, 2941.51

STATE	SITUATIONS IN WHICH ASSIGNABLE	WHEN ASSIGNED	WHOSE INSTANCE	COMPEN-SATION	CITATION
Oklahoma	all cases in which defendant arraigned (public defender in Tulsa and Oklahoma counties)	on arraignment	mandatory on request	max. of $100 each for up to 2 att'ys[29]	Okla. Stat. Ann. 1937, tit. 19, §§134 to 134e; tit. 22, §§464, 1271; Okla. Sess. Laws 1957, Ch. 5b, §2
Oregon	a) criminal cases in circuit court	on arraignment	mandatory on request	misd., guilty plea: $5; misd., not guilty plea: $10/ day (2 days only); fel., guilty plea: $15/day (2 days only); fel., not guilty plea: $15/ day (3 days only); homicide: max. $150	Ore. Rev. Stat. 1955, §§135.310, 135.320, 135.330, 138.820, 138.840
	b) appeals in capital cases	no provision	mandatory	reasonable, determined by Supreme Court	
Pennsylvania	capital cases[30]	after indictment	mandatory	max. of $500 each for up to 2 att'ys plus expenses	Pa. Stats. Ann. 1957, Tit. 19, §§783, 784

State	Cases	When appointed	Mandatory	Compensation	Citation
Rhode Island	cases referred by super. courts (public defender)	no provision	no provision	salary	R. I. Gen. Laws 1956, §§12-15-1 through 12-15-7
South Carolina	capital cases	when before trial court	mandatory on request	no provision	S. C. Code 1952, §§17-506, 17-507
South Dakota	any criminal case in cir., mun. or city courts	whenever shown that def. cannot employ counsel	mandatory on request	homicide: max. $100; all others: max. $50; appeals: add. allow. to $100	S. D. Code 1939, §§34.1901, 34-3506
Tennessee	a) all crimes and misdemeanors[31]	no provision	mandatory on request	no provision	Tenn. Code Ann. 1956, §§40-121, 40-2001 to 40-2003
	b) all cases in Gen. Sess. Courts and similar courts	on arraignment or trial	mandatory on request or when required	no provision	
Texas	a) capital cases	on arraignment	mandatory	in felony case after def. has attested to his indigency and fact that he has not been released on bail, up to $10/day in court and $25 for a "bona fide" appeal	Tex. Code Ann. 1954, §§494, 494a
	b) felony	no provision	discretion of court		

STATE	SITUATIONS IN WHICH ASSIGNABLE	WHEN ASSIGNED	WHOSE INSTANCE	COMPENSATION	CITATION
Utah	cases in which defendant arraigned	on arraignment	mandatory on request	none	Utah Code Ann. 1953, §77-22-12
Vermont	crimes punishable by penitentiary sentence	no provision	discretion of court	discretion of court	Vt. Rev. Stat. 1947, Tit. 9, §2397; Sup. Ct. Rule 16
Virginia	felony and certain other cases (public defender in certain cities)	before def. pleads or waives a jury	discretion of court except where fel. when mandatory	if pun. by death or impris. for over 10 years, up to $100; other fel. up to $20	Va. Code Ann. 1950, §§14-181, 19-166, 19-214.1, 19-7, 19-7.1
Washington	criminal cases in superior court[32]	before arraignment	mandatory on request	in fel. cases, up to $25/day per counsel (not more than 2) while employed on trial, and $25 per counsel for preparing for trial or plea	Wash. Rev. Code 1956, §§10.01.-110, 10.40.030, 10.46.050
West Virginia	felonies and misdemeanors	after indictment	mandatory after indictment otherwise mandatory on request	misd.: max. of $25; fel.: max. of $50	W. Va. Code Ann. 1955, §6190; Const. of W. Va.; Rule 4, Rules of Practice, Trial Court

Wisconsin	a) felonies and writs of hab. corp.	arraignment	mandatory on request	discretion of court based on customary fees or may be max. $25 each ½ day in ct.; $15 each ½ day preparation up to 5 days; $15 each ½ day at deposition; plus certain disbursements	Wis. Stat. Ann. 1958, §§957.26, 256.49
	b) appeal or pros. of writ of error	no provision	discretionary on request		
Wyoming	a) felonies and cases presented by indict. or info.	at preliminary hearing or arraignment	mandatory on request	misd.: $15–$50; fel.: $25–$100; capital: $50–$200.	Wyo. Comp. Stat. Ann. 1945, §§10–805, 10–806, 10–806A–C, 15–107a
	b) appeals to supreme court	when before sup. court	discretion of ct.	discretion of sup. ct.	

1. Letter from the Chief Justice of the United States to Orison S. Marden, President, National Legal Aid Association, dated October 10, 1956. Reprinted in XV (No. 2) The Legal Aid Brief Case (1956), p. 27.

2. It has been suggested that the constitutional right to counsel "becomes meaningless when the prisoner [arrested by federal authorities] cannot afford to hire a lawyer to give him the help which he needs before appearing in the Commissioner's office." *Statement of The Committee on the Bill of Rights of the American Bar Association* (1944), pp. 47–48. The same can be said for prisoners who are arrested by state authorities and are unable to obtain counsel during hearings before police and magistrates' courts, especially if the particular state by statute or constitution fails to afford the "right" to such assistance at that stage in the proceedings. For, in either event, statements and admissions unwisely, inadvertently, and even erroneously made by the accused can be used against him later at his trial. See, generally, cases collected in *People* v. *Steinmetz*, 240 N. Y. 411 (1925).

3. Of course, it may well be impossible, as a practical matter, to supply counsel to indigents at or near the time of arrest. Yet there has been a growing recognition of the need for some such provision in order to make individual safeguards meaningful from the very inception of a conflict with state authority. Such recognition has, for example, led to the publication, jointly by The Association of the Bar of the City of New York and the New York Civil Liberties Union, of a pamphlet for popular distribution entitled *If You Are Arrested . . .* (1955), setting forth answers to such questions as: What are your rights? What can you do? Where can you get help? What does the law say you cannot do?

4. The problem of cross-examination of witnesses for the prosecution illustrates one aspect of the situation faced by the layman defending himself. Cross-examination, which we depend upon as one of the principal instruments for the determination of truth in judicial proceedings, is a matter of great difficulty and subtlety. A good example of the importance of this legal tool, and the difficulties involved in its uses, is contained in Edgar Lustgarten's account of Governor Robinson's cross-examination of Bridget Sullivan, the Irish maid, in the celebrated Lizzie Borden murder case. Lustgarten, *Verdict in Dispute* (1950), pp. 251–53.

5. Some of the pitfalls faced by the unrepresented defendant are poignantly illustrated by the trial of one Gibbs for larceny. See *Gibbs* v. *Burke*, 337 U. S. 773 (1949).

Gibbs was indicted for larcency and receiving stolen goods. He neither requested a lawyer nor was advised of his right to be assigned one. Upon a plea of not guilty, he was tried before a jury and convicted. In its opinion reversing the conviction, the United States Supreme Court made many references to the improper conduct of the trial. A colloquy not mentioned by the Supreme Court, however, would seem to sum up the defendants inability to protect himself. After commenting that he had no witnesses to offer on his behalf, the record shows the following:

The Court: Do you wish to argue it to the jury? You may, if you want to.

The Defendant: No, sir; I don't believe so. I am not educated to talk to the people. Gibbs v. Burke, supra, *Record on Certiorari, pp. 31–32.*

6. The trend "has been away from fixed sentences prescribed by statute or fixed by the court, in favor of quasi-indeterminate sentences with fixed upper limits subject to downward adjustment by parole or sentencing boards." Dession, *Criminal Law, Administration and Public Order* (1948), pp. 56, 194. In the *Report to the Judicial Conference of the Committee on Punishment for Crime* (1942), it was stated, p. 4:

The indeterminate sentence is an effort to make punishment truly reformative. Its theory is that one who has been guilty of serious infraction of the criminal laws should be imprisoned for such time as is necessary to cure him of his antisocial tendencies and should then be conditionally released under parole, with adequate supervision, for such time as is necessary to restore him to the normal life of a law-abiding citizen of the community.

See also Brecher and Brecher, "Why Judges Can't Sleep," The Saturday Evening Post, p. 25 (July 13, 1957).

This trend has been accompanied by a growing emphasis on the rehabilitation of the individual as the primary purpose of the criminal process:

Since deterrence is at best a negative control, segregation effective only so long as it continues, and retribution merely retaliatory rather than corrective in aim, penological experts now believe that treatment which places primary emphasis upon reformation renders maximum service to the community. Comment, "Reform in Federal Penal Procedure: The Federal Corrections and Parole Improvement Bills," 53 Yale L. J. 773 (1944).

7. 287 U. S. 45, 69 (1932).

8. Morgan, *Some Problems of Proof Under the Anglo-American System of Litigation* (1956), p. 3.

9. *Id.* at 9.

10. *Williams* v. *Kaiser*, 323 U. S. 471, 476 (1945).

11. *Powell* v. *Alabama*, 287 U. S. 45, 61 (1932).

12. Mannheim, *Criminal Justice and Social Reconstruction* (1946), p. 2.

13. *Adams* v. *United States* ex rel. *McCann*, 317 U. S. 269, 279 (1942).

14. The overt manifestation of the purge is, of course, the public confessional trial, aimed at popular political education rather than "justice." Here, significantly, defense counsel serves no function whatsoever, since the principal roles are assigned to the prosecution and the "cringing penitent." See Dewar, "The Moscow Trials Revised," 6 *Problems of Communism* (1957), pp. 46, 47.

   Even more significant, however, is the fact that the purge's covert operation dispenses altogether with the pretense of trial, and of course with both the form and substance of defense. Despite the silence shrouding this vastly more important and widespread side of the purge—which is the aftermath of the public trial of the selected confessors—its operation has been fully detailed and exposed. See, generally, Brezezinski, *The Permanent Purge* (1956).

15. Frank, J., dissenting in *United States* v. *Johnson*, 238 F. 2d 565, 572–73 (2d Cir. 1956), *rev'd*, 352 U.S. 565 (1957).

16. Brownell, *Legal Aid in the United States* (1951), p. 83; see Tweed, *The Legal Aid Society, New York City, 1876–1951* (1954), pp. 87, 97; see also Appendix.

17. Callagy, "Legal Aid in Criminal Cases," 42 J. Crim. L., Crim. & P. S. 589, 594 (1952). Questionnaires were sent to localities in every state and some of the territories of the United States. Judge Callagy stated, "The questionnaires disclose the fact that of the total who answered, 118 stated that in their experience, defendants accused of felonies were not represented (a few stated that a minor number were unrepresented), and 175 stated that the same was true of defendants charged with misdemeanors." *Ibid.*

18. See Appendix.

19. Speech before 75th Anniversary Dinner of The Legal Aid Society of New York (1951).

Notes to Chapter II

1. See Becker and Heidelbaugh, "The Right to Counsel in Criminal Cases," XXVIII Notre Dame Lawyer 351, 355 (1953).

2. Letter from Sir Francis Walsingham to Sir Edward Stafford, quoted in Steuart, *Trial of Mary Queen of Scots* (2d ed. 1951), p. 192.

3. Mary's education was French. Later she became fluent in Scots and, after her imprisonment in England, she studied English. See Steuart, *Trial of Mary Queen of Scots* (2d ed. 1951), pp. 29–30.

4. 7 and 8 William III, c. 3, s. 1 (1695). The statute, which became effective in 1696, provided that in treason and misprison of treason cases counsel could be retained by defendants and that:

    . . . [I]n case any person or persons so accused or indicted shall desire counsel the court before whom such person or persons shall be tried, or some judge of that court, shall and is hereby authorised and required immediately, upon his or their request, to assign to such person and persons such and so many counsel, not exceeding two, as the person or persons shall desire. . . .

5. See Beaney, *The Right to Counsel in American Courts* (1955), pp. 9–11.

6. 1 Stephen, *A History of the Criminal Law of England* (1883), p. 424. The same point is made by J. Chitty in his work, 1 Chitty, *A Practical Treatise on the Criminal Law* (1819), p. 278:

    Even, upon the general issue, the strict rule of law against defending by counsel, has been considerably modified by modern practice. For, at the present day, a prisoner is allowed counsel to instruct him what questions to ask, or even to ask questions for him with respect to matters of fact, and to cross examine the witnesses for the crown, and to examine those produced on the part of the defendant, though not to address the jury. And in case of mere misdemeanours, or any offenses less than felony, it does not appear that the right of the party indicted to a full defence by advocates, has ever been disputed.

7. 6 and 7 William IV, c. 114, s. 1 (1836). This statute provided in part that:

    All persons tried for felonies shall be admitted, after the close of the case for the prosecution, to make full answer and defense thereto by counsel learned in the law, or by attorney in courts where attornies practise as counsel.

8. 4 Blackstone, *Commentaries* (14th ed. 1803), p. 355. Sir James
    Stephen, writing many years later, made the same point.

    *A criminal trial in those days was not unlike a race between
    the King and the prisoner, in which the King had a long start
    and the prisoner was heavily weighted. . . . He was not allowed
    as a matter of right, but only as an occasional, exceptional
    favour, to have either counsel or solicitors to advise him as to
    his defence, or to see his witnesses and put their evidence in
    order. When he came into court he was set to fight for his
    life with absolutely no knowledge of the evidence to be pro-
    duced against him. . . . That an uneducated man, whose life is
    at stake, and who has no warning of what is to be said against
    him, should do himself justice on such an occasion is a moral
    impossibility. But this was what was required of every person
    tried for high treason in the seventeenth century. . . . 1 Stephen,
    A History of the Criminal Law of England* (1883), pp. 397–98.

9. This was the conclusion reached by Mr. Justice Sutherland
    writing for the majority in *Powell* v. *Alabama*, 287 U. S. 47, 61
    (1932). Professor William M. Beaney apparently disagrees. See
    Beaney, *The Right to Counsel in American Courts* (1955), p. 16
    et seq.

10. See the state constitutions cited in *Powell* v. *Alabama*, 287 U. S.
    45, 61–65 (1932).

11. 2 Swift, *A System of the Laws of the State of Connecticut* (1796),
    p. 399, quoted in *Powell* v. *Alabama*, 287 U. S. 45, 63–64
    (1932).

    In *United States* v. *Hare*, 2 Wheeler's Criminal Cases 283, 292
    (U. S. Cir. Ct. Balt. 1818), counsel for the defense made the
    following statement when challenged as to his right to advise a
    client to stand mute:

    *The gentleman has charged us with obstructing the course
    of justice, and vehemently asks if such conduct is to be tolerated
    here, which in the courts of Great Britain would subject us to
    fine and imprisonment. Sir, I deny the law to be so in England
    as he stated it, and whenever he feels disposed to enter into
    that question, shall be ready to meet him; but if it were so there,
    I desire to bless God and those who purchased our inestimable
    privileges with their blood, that our situation in this court is not
    so humble and degraded. Has the gentleman forgotten, sir, that
    while in England, the accused is denied the aid of counsel
    altogether, except on questions of law, and then receives it as
    pure bounty from the court—here, he has a legal—nay, a con-
    stitutional right to be heard and advised by counsel in every
    stage of the proceedings against him; that while in the criminal
    courts of England the counsel for the prisoner is the mere*

creature, the automaton, the very serf *of the court, holding his place by a base and servile tenure—here, he is an independent officer of the constitution, standing erect and firm on his constitutional freehold, and accountable to God and his conscience alone for whatever advice he may give his client. Execrated let him be, and forever abhorred by his professional brethren, who shall meanly shrink from the sacred duties he has to perform, or tamely suffer the interposition of any judge or court between him and his client. Sir, we have deemed it a legal right of the prisoners to refuse to plead; we have thought it might be beneficial to them; and with these impressions, if we had not advised, or having advised, were afraid to avow it, should we not merit the blasting mildew of public reproach which would inevitably fall upon us after the warring passions of the multitude against these prisoners shall have abated. We have advised our clients to insist on every legal advantage in defence of their lives, and here openly avow it, fearless of consequences. Our object is to save them from punishment, if not* legally *obnoxious to it, whatever may be their* moral *guilt; and this cannot be censured in counsel but by those whose unhallowed thirst for blood must be slaked in spite of the constitution and the laws of their country.*

12. Act Regulating Proceedings and Trials in Criminal Cases, §2 (N. J. Mar. 6, 1795). This statute applied to all defendants under indictment whether the case was capital or not.

13. Laws of New Hampshire (Melcher 1792) 247–248.

14. See *Johnson v. Zerbst*, 304 U. S. 458, 463 (1938), where the Court said:

   The Sixth Amendment withholds from federal courts, in all criminal proceedings, the power and authority to deprive an accused of his life or liberty unless he has or waives the assistance of counsel. . . .

   Rule 44 of the Federal Rules of Criminal Procedure provides:

   If the defendant appears in court without counsel, the court shall advise him of his right to counsel and assign counsel to represent him at every stage of the proceeding unless he elects to proceed without counsel or is able to obtain counsel.

   See also *Walker v. Johnston*, 312 U. S. 275 (1941).

15. See *Williams v. Kaiser*, 323 U. S. 471 (1945); *Tomkins v. Missouri*, 323 U. S. 485 (1945).

16. In state courts, the right of the indigent to have counsel appointed, as the Supreme Court indicated in *Powell v. Alabama*, 287 U. S. 45 (1932), is one of the fundamental elements of a

fair trial where the charge is a capital offense. Even in non-capital cases, where the right is qualified, the fairness of the trial depends on whether an adequate defense without counsel was possible. See *Betts* v. *Brady*, 316 U. S. 45 (1942); *Townsend* v. *Burke*, 334 U. S. 736 (1948).

17. See Appendix.

18. Beaney, *The Right to Counsel in American Courts* (1955), p. 225.

19. Maguire, *The Lance of Justice* (1928), p. 10.

20. *Ibid.*

21. Smith, "Commentaries," *The Metropolis in Modern Life* (Fisher ed. 1955), p. 307.

22. Brownell, *Legal Aid in the United States* (1951), p. 35.

23. One is in Philadelphia, another in Boston, and the third in Springfield, Massachusetts.

24. "The Necessity and Advisability of Creating the Office of Public Defender," *Fifth Report of the Law Reform Committee of The Association of the Bar of the City of New York* (1915), pp. 4-5. The function of the Oklahoma Public Defender was the legal representation of minors, delinquents, orphans and defectives. See Smith, *Justice and the Poor* (1919), p. 117, n. 1.

25. The State of California has provided for the establishment of a public-defender office in any county which desires this type of service. *Cal. Gov't Code,* §§27700-27711. In addition, where a public defender is not available, assigned counsel are compensated by the State on an individual-case basis. Thirty-eight counties of varying sizes rely entirely on the assignment system. Twenty counties, some urban and others rural, use the assignment and defender system in conjunction, paying court-appointed attorneys for cases refused by public defenders because of conflict of interest or for any other reason.

The public-defender offices of Los Angeles and Alameda Counties are among the oldest offices in the state. They are substantially alike. In both offices the public defenders and their staffs are selected by civil service examination. Private practice is not allowed. In both counties, as well as in San Francisco, provision has been made for the representation of indigents charged with misdemeanors as well as felonies. For historic reasons, Los Angeles County has separate county and city public defenders which together cover all criminal courts within the county. Two city public defenders, those of Los Angeles and Long Beach, defend misdemeanors and handle the preliminary stages of felonies. The county public defender handles the final stages of felony cases in those cities, and defends felony charges from the beginning in the remaining portions of the county.

26. Bliss, *Directory of Public Defenders* (1956).

27. *The Statistical Abstract of the United States* (U. S. Dept. of Commerce 1955), p. 7.

28. Smith, *Justice and the Poor* (1919), p. 103.

29. Pound, "Social and Economic Problems of the Law," CXXXVI Annals 2 (March 1928). In this connection, it should be noted that, particularly in California, the growth of the public defender idea went hand in hand with governmental and judicial reform. See Flack, "Notes on Current Legislation," American Political Science Review (1913), p. 411; Gray, "The Conduct of Trials in the Courts; Some Radical Suggestions for Reform," The Recorder (San Francisco, July 28, 1913). See also "The Poor Man in Court," XV Transactions of the Commonwealth Club of California (1920), p. 119.

30. See Smith, *Justice and the Poor* (1919), p. 116:

> . . . [T]*he defender idea, in last analysis, is nothing more revolutionary than a plea for the extension of what is best in the assignment system and for reorganization along modern lines of efficiency. As payment of a reasonable sum for services and expenses in murder cases has worked well, let it be extended to the other cases, for assignments in all cases rest on the same principle and are used to secure the same result. As centralization of work makes for economy, efficiency, and responsibility, let there be, instead of a shifting group of attorneys, one definite official or organization charged with the duty of defending the poor, to whom all assignments may be made.*

31. 287 U. S. 45 (1932).

32. *Id.* at 68.

Notes to Chapter III

1. All of these field studies, except one, were conducted by the committee staff. The report on the assigned-counsel system in Tompkins County, New York, was prepared by Professor Bertram F. Willcox and Mr. Edward J. Bloustein of the Cornell Law School.

2. See Appendix.

3. Counsel is generally assigned at the time of arraignment when the defendant enters his plea to the charge against him. In most States there is some question as to the defendant's constitutional right to counsel prior to arraignment in the trial court. See

Beaney, *The Right to Counsel in American Courts* (1955), p. 127. Furthermore, where there is a statutory requirement in a state that counsel be assigned it is, in most instances, not operative before indictment.

4. At the worst, the basis of assignment may be haphazard and the counsel assigned of the very lowest quality. Federal Judge Edward J. Dimock commented upon the selection of counsel under the traditional system as he observed it in New York City some years ago:

> *When I came to the Bar in New York, a row of seedy characters, hardly distinguishable from the prisoners, used to sit on the front bench in the Court of General Sessions. When an accused person would appear before the judge for pleading and state that he had no money to pay counsel, the judge would announce 'I will appoint Mr. X to represent you' and the first of the row of seedy characters would engage the accused in earnest conference in the back of the courtroom. The conference would ostensibly concern the facts of the case but, in reality, was a searching inquiry rather similar to an examination in proceedings supplementary to execution, designed to disclose any assets possessed by the accused or his relatives or friends. The percentage of guilty pleas was much higher in the cases where the search proved fruitless.* Dimock, "The Public Defender: A Step Toward a Police State?," 42 A.B.A. J. 219–20 (1956).

5. See p. 65, *infra*.

6. No provision for the payment of counsel assigned in non-capital cases is found in twenty-seven states. Most of the remaining states provide only token payments which are grossly unremunerative for the services performed. Frequently the payments do not cover the expenses of counsel. Examples may be found in the provisions in South Dakota, Texas, and Virginia. The allowance in some states may be adequate depending, of course, on the amount of work required of the attorney and on the local fee scale. There is a trend in the new state legislation relating to the assignment of counsel toward leaving the amount of compensation to the trial court. In California, Colorado, Indiana, Maine, and Michigan, for example the fee may be set by the court with no statutory limit prescribed.

7. In a few jurisdictions, law students or law clerks are available to assist assigned counsel in legal research and investigation. Trained investigators are, on the other hand, never provided by the state and are available only if the assigned attorney is willing to pay for them out of his own pocket.

8. *Powell* v. *Alabama*, 287 U. S. 45 (1932); *Williams* v. *Kaiser*, 323 U. S. 471 (1945); *Tomkins* v. *Missouri*, 323 U. S. 485 (1945).

9. See Appendix.

10. Calif. Pen. Code, §1241; N. Y. Code of Cr. Proc., §§308, 308a.

11. Survey conducted by the staff of the Special Committee to Study Defender Systems in Essex County, New Jersey during the summer of 1956. Questionnaires were sent to all members of the Essex County Bar Association. A "typical" attorney for the purposes of calculating the number of assignments is actually most difficult to pinpoint due to new admissions to the Bar, movement of attorneys from one county to another, and the lack of a completely uniform assignment procedure from one judge to another. The statistics compiled by the committee's staff from the Essex County, New Jersey (750 questionnaires were analyzed), survey reveal that, when questioned as to the number of assignments received since 1950, 726 attorneys replied as follows: 105 had received no assignments; 127 had received one; 180 had received two; 142 had received three; 58 had received four; 41 had received five; and 48 had received more than five.

12. The Habeas Corpus Advisory Committee is composed of approximately 400 members of the Junior Section of the New Jersey State Bar Association. Provision for such committees is made in Rule 1:12–9(c) of *The Revision of the Rules Governing the Courts of the State of New Jersey* (1953).

13. There are three other examples of this type now in operation in the United States. They are found in Cincinnati, New Orleans and Pittsburgh.

14. Boston and Springfield, Massachusetts and Philadelphia are the only examples of this type now operating in the United States. The name of the Philadelphia organization has been recently changed to Defender Association of Philadelphia.

15. As a matter of practice, voluntary-defender organizations generally do not accept assignments in capital cases where the State pays a fee to assigned counsel.

16. The total salaries (legal, stenographic, and investigative) for the Criminal Courts Branch of the New York Legal Aid Society in 1957 amounted to $144,900. This figure does not represent all the costs, however. In view of the fact that the Civil and Criminal Courts Branches of the New York Legal Aid Society are integrated for the purpose of administration and fund raising, a certain percentage of the central office's expenses are attributed to the cost of operating the Criminal Courts Branch. At the beginning of 1957 there were 22 attorneys in the Criminal Courts Branch, 1 investigator, and 7 clerical and secretarial personnel. At the end of 1957 there were 24 attorneys one of whom did some investigative work, and 2 full-time investigators.

The 1955–56 budget of the Philadelphia Voluntary Defender Association (its fiscal year is June 1 to May 31) was $66,080.92. As of June 1957, its staff consisted of 5 lawyers, 4 investigators, and 5 clerical and secretarial personnel.

The above figures do not reflect the service performed by volunteer attorneys or law students. See note 20, Ch. III, *infra*.

17. The Legal Aid Society of New York conducts its own fund-raising campaign and also shares in the proceeds of the campaigns of the Greater New York Fund. The society receives strong support from the New York Bar.

18. Both the Boston and the Philadelphia voluntary defender offices are almost exclusively dependent on the local community chests for financial support. Neither of these offices engages in extensive independent fund-raising activities as is done by the New York Legal Aid Society.

19. See note 16, Ch. III, *supra*.

20. Boston makes significant use of volunteers. The Harvard Voluntary Defenders Committee, composed of 26 second and third year law students, performs virtually all initial jail interviews and the bulk of the investigatory work. No full-time investigators are retained by the parent organization, the Voluntary Defenders Committee, Inc. of Boston. The Philadelphia office also utilizes volunteers, but to a lesser extent. Each month one of the large Philadelphia firms supplies the full-time services of one of its junior attorneys. Law students from the local law schools perform interviewing and investigating tasks. In New York City most appellate work is referred to a committee of volunteer attorneys and some of the larger law firms donate the services of younger attorneys to the Criminal Courts Branch of the New York Legal Aid Society. The latter act as investigators and attorneys, serving usually for 30-day periods.

21. The starting salary of lawyers employed by the New York City Legal Aid Society in 1957 was $3,200. The highest paid assistant defender on its staff as of June 1957 received $7,650. In Boston the annual starting salary for attorneys is $2,000. Assistant defenders in the Philadelphia office commence their employment with a salary of $4,200. The highest salary paid as of June 1957 to an assistant defender in that office was $5,600.

22. In Illinois an indigent defendant has the choice of the public defender or other counsel appointed by the courts. *Ill. Ann. Stat.* 1957, Ch. 34, §163f.

23. There are marked contrasts in operating procedures between the larger public-defender offices and the single-lawyer offices. To handle their high case load, the larger offices have established

regular operating procedures, which regulate the work of attorneys as well as clerical personnel. In commenting upon this fact, Mr. George Nye, the Public Defender of Alameda County, California, wrote in his *Report to the Board of Supervisors for the Fiscal Year 1955–56*, p. 6: "In view of these demands upon us, it is fortunate that we enjoy the advantages of centralization and specialization. For these reasons, among others, a surprising degree of efficiency has been achieved."

The procedures of the Alameda County Office have been codified in an office manual which prescribes the duties and responsibilities of the deputy defenders in processing a case.

On the other hand, the work load of many one-lawyer offices is handled on a case-by-case basis in the same manner as the defender's private law business. In fact, the "public defender's office" is frequently the private law office of the part-time defender.

24. For example, the Public Defender of Los Angeles County had as of 1956 a staff consisting of twenty-four deputies, one lieutenant and four investigators. See Bliss, *Defense Investigation* (1956), p. 18.

25. Most public-defender offices do not have a trained investigator on their staff. The county public defenders in Connecticut must make a special request to the Chief Justice of the Supreme Court of Errors to obtain funds to pay for an investigation. See note 27, Ch. V, *infra*.

Several public-defender offices look to the prosecutor's investigators for assistance. In this category are the public defenders of Marin County, California, and Tazewell County, Illinois. The latter has recently commented on this procedure: "Theoretically we have the use of the sheriff's office [for investigation]. Practically this is very unsatisfactory." *Public Defenders* (Institute of Judicial Administration, New York, May 18, 1956), p. 12.

26. In two counties in California the public defenders and the assistant defenders are selected on the basis of competitive civil service examination. The public defenders in Connecticut are appointed by the judges of the Superior Court. Election by popular vote occurs in Omaha and San Francisco.

27. For example, the following chart indicates the experience of the assistant defenders in the office of the Public Defender in Chicago as of 1956:

ASSISTANT DEFENDER	PREVIOUS LEGAL EXPERIENCE	YEAR OF APPOINTMENT
A.	'49–'51 —Investigator on Public Defender Staff	'51
B.	'50–'52 —Bail Bond Investigator, Dept. of Commerce, Illinois	'52
C.	'47–'50 —Investigator on Public Defender Staff	'50
D.	'50–'55 —Election Attorney, Cook Cty.	'55
E.	Six months private practice	'54
F.	Private practice—over 500 criminal cases	'31
G.	'50–'53 —Private practice	'53
H.	Police Dept. '50–'52 —Investigator, Office of Price Stabilization.	'52

Many of the public defenders in the single-lawyer office of Connecticut have been reappointed annually for years. The former Public Defender for the New Haven District in Connecticut, who died in 1957, held the position for many years.

28. The Public Defender of Alameda County, California, for example, has a suite of eight offices, including a library, in the Alameda County Court Building. His staff may also use county automobiles to aid in investigation of cases or to allow a member of the staff to represent indigents in the various far flung towns of the County. See also *Ill. Rev. Stat.*, Ch. 34, §163i (State Bar Ass'n Ed. 1957).

29. See *Public Defenders* (Institute of Judicial Administration, New York, May 18, 1956), p. 15.

30. Most public defenders submit a yearly budget request to a local governing body. See *Id.*, at pp. 22–23.

31. The annual retainer paid to each Connecticut public defender is expected to cover almost all of his overhead expenses. See note 25, Ch. III, *supra*. The funds for all public defenders are originally appropriated by the Connecticut Legislature to the Judicial Department of the State which then provides for payments to the individual defender.

32. The Rochester Legal Aid Society for civil cases was established

in 1911 as a department of a social agency. It later became an independent society with its own board of directors.

33. N. Y. County Law, §224(10). This statute provides:

    The board of supervisors of any county having a population of over two hundred thousand may appropriate such sums of money as it may deem proper toward the maintenance of a private legal aid bureau or society organized and operating for the aid or relief of needy persons residing within the county.

34. For a description of the Puerto Rican system, see address by former Chief Justice A. Cecil Snyder of the Supreme Court of Puerto Rico before 34th Annual Meeting of the National Legal Aid Association, quoted in XV (No. 2) The Legal Aid Brief Case (1956), pp. 60–61.

Notes to Chapter IV

1. N. Y. Correction Law, §203.

2. No defender system need provide the most distinguished members of the bar as counsel. But, on the other hand, no defender system serves its true purpose unless it affords representation which is experienced, competent, and zealous. Judge Edgerton of the United States Court of Appeals for the District of Columbia, has forcefully stated that representation by inexperienced or negligent counsel cannot be considered to be adequate representation:

    In the circumstances the failure of counsel to produce all available evidence, in a case involving the life of the accused, should not be held against him [the accused]. It would be a strange system of law which first assigned inexperienced or negligent counsel in a capital case and then made counsel's neglect a ground for refusing a new trial. The right to counsel is not formal, but substantial. It is hard to ask experienced counsel, of proved ability, to serve in cases of this sort without compensation; but the rights of poor persons can be protected in no other way until systematic provision is made for their defense. Johnson v. United States, 110 F. 2d 562, 563 (D.C. Cir. 1940); *see also* Baldwin v. United States, 141 F. Supp. 310 (E.D.S.C. 1956).

3. *United States* v. *Ah Kee Eng,* 241 F. 2d 157, 161 (2d Cir. 1957).

4. *Public Defenders* (Institute of Judicial Administration, New York, May 18, 1956), pp. 21–22.

5. Bliss, *Defense Investigation* (1956), pp. 28, 29.

6. *United States* v. *Johnson,* 238 F. 2d 565, 572 (2d Cir. 1956), *rev'd,* 352 U. S. 565 (1957).

7. In Ex Parte *Sullivan*, 107 F. Supp. 514, 517–18 (D. Utah 1952), it was said:

> *Petitioners were entitled to have effective counsel at the trial. The question here is how they ever could have had effective counsel at the trial, no matter how skilled, in view of what went on before trial. They were denied effective counsel at the trial itself because of what went on before trial while the defendants were without counsel, and absolutely under the control of the prosecution.*
>
> *The time a defendant needs counsel most is immediately after his arrest and until trial. . . .*
>
> *Indeed, counsel was not appointed for them until after they had been arraigned and had entered their pleas of not guilty. By that time the evidence was all neatly tied up for delivery at the trial. . . . One can imagine a cynical prosecutor saying: "Let them have the most illustrious counsel, now. They can't escape the noose. There is nothing that counsel can do for them at the trial."*

8. In re *Groban*, 352 U. S. 330, 349–50 (1957).

9. *. . . the right to assistance by counsel means effective assistance by an attorney who gives the accused his complete loyalty and whose service is of such character as to preserve the essential integrity of the proceedings.* In re York, 283 P. 2d 567, 570 (Okla. Cr. 1955), cert. denied, York v. McLeod, 350 U. S. 839 (1955).

The obligations of assigned counsel have been equated with those of retained counsel. In the case of *Downer* v. *Dunaway*, 53 F. 2d 586, 589 (5th Cir. 1931), for example, the court stated:

> *It goes without saying that an accused who is unable by reason of poverty to employ counsel is entitled to be defended in all his rights as fully and to the same extent as is an accused who is able to employ his own counsel to represent him.*

The relation between the assigned attorney and the defendant is the same where the assigned counsel is a public defender. In a recent California decision it was stated that:

> *The circumstance that . . . [the defendant's] counsel was a deputy public defender is not one of significance to the constitutional question we are considering. The source of his compensation is different, but otherwise the relation of attorney and client is the same when a public defender appears for one accused of crime as would be the relation between privately employed counsel and client.* People v. Agnew, 114 Cal. App. 2d 841, 845, 250 P. 2d 369, 371 (1952).

Notes to Chapter V

1. This conclusion is based upon the general investigation made by the committee as well as upon a report of the assigned-counsel system in Tompkins County, New York. This report, which was dated March 23, 1957, was prepared, at the request of the committee, by Professor Bertram F. Willcox and Doctor Edward J. Bloustein, both of whom are associated with the Law School of Cornell University. Their report notes the following practice with respect to non-indictable offenses:

   Outside the city [Ithaca], the problem is more obstinate. The justices make no attempt to assign counsel. They say that they have no power to assign. Furthermore, the practical difficulties are too great. There are few attorneys in the towns and villages. Besides, the justice, who is not himself a lawyer, would feel hesitant to call on a lawyer to render free professional services. And many lawyers doubt a justice's authority to assign them. P. 10.

2. *The Revision of the Rules Governing the Courts of the State of New Jersey* (1953), Rule 1:12–9.

3. *Report of Junior Section Committee on Indigent Criminal Representation,* 80 N.J.L.J. Index 237, 245 (1957).

4. A committee of the New Jersey Bar Association has proposed that this be accomplished through a revision of Rule 1:12–9.

5. N.Y.C. *Magistrates' Courts Annual Report* (1955), p. 42. In New York City the lowest court of original criminal jurisdiction is the Magistrates' Court. There are 23 Parts of the Magistrates' Court operating in the Borough of Manhattan.

6. See Dash, "Cracks in the Foundation of Criminal Justice," 46 Ill. L. Rev. 385, 389 (1951).

7. *Report of Junior Section Committee on Indigent Criminal Representation, supra,* note 3, Ch. V, at 245.

8. See Kadish and Kimball, "Legal Representation of the Indigent in Criminal Cases in Utah," 4 Utah L. Rev. 198 (1954).

9. The results obtained through a questionnaire submitted by the staff of this committee to the members of Essex County Bar Association in the summer of 1956 indicate that a very small percentage of those who answered the questionnaire had handled extensive criminal work prior to their first assigned case. 653 attorneys answered the question, "Did you handle any criminal work prior to your first non-capital assignment? If so, was it extensive?" The results were as follows:

		PERCENT
Total Who Answered:	653	100.0
Any Criminal Work:	371	56.6
Extensive Work:	62	9.5
No Criminal Work:	282	43.4

The survey by questionnaire conducted by Professor Willcox in Tompkins County, New York, shows that a somewhat higher percentage of the Bar of that county had some criminal experience prior to their first assigned case. Thirty attorneys in Tompkins County responded to the question, "How many such retained criminal cases, if any, had you handled before handling your first assigned case?" The results were as follows:

NUMBER OF RETAINED CASES PRIOR TO FIRST ASSIGNED CASE	NUMBER OF ATTORNEYS
None	Ten
1–2	Seven
3–5	Nine
Over 5	Four

10. Professor Willcox and Doctor Bloustein report what seems to be a general lack of concern among the Bar of Tompkins County with the question of timely representation. They circulated a questionnaire to the Bar and of the 36 responses received, "only three answered that the usual time of assigning counsel is too late." Professor Willcox and Doctor Bloustein go on to observe "that these three represent half of the criminal experience of the County, in terms of number of cases handled from 1954 through 1956."

11. See *Report on the Assigned Counsel System in New Jersey* (New Jersey Administrative Office of the Courts, 1955), p. 7.

12. *The Revision of the Rules Governing the Courts of the State of New Jersey* (1953), Rule 1:12–9(a).

Another example of an attempt to provide counsel to indigents charged with serious crimes as soon as possible after arrest is found in Wyoming. A recent Wyoming statute provides:

If it shall appear at any preliminary hearing upon a felony charge before a Justice of the Peace, that the person so charged is without counsel and unable to employ counsel, said Justice of the Peace, upon request of the accused for counsel shall immediately certify such fact to the judge of the District Court of his county, who shall forthwith certify to said Justice of the Peace the appointment of competent counsel. . . .

This statute also provides that except for admission to bail, all proceedings in the Justice of the Peace court should be stayed until the appointment of counsel has been certified by the District Court. Wy. Comp. Stat. Ann. 1945, §15–107A.

13. See p. 50, *supra*. In commenting upon the assignment practice in New Jersey, the *Report of Junior Section Committee on Indigent Criminal Representation, supra*, note 3, Ch. V, at 245, stated:

> *There is considerable overlapping in the assignment program in that generally assignment is made for trial purposes only and that actions to correct illegal sentence or obtain habeas corpus as a practical matter require assignment of a counsellor of law who is generally a complete stranger to the original proceedings. No one will dispute that the trial counsel is best qualified to prosecute Appellate matters and therefore the assignment should continue until final disposition of all phases of the case is had.*

14. See note 11, Ch. III, *supra*.

15. Letter from Chief Justice Arthur T. Vanderbilt to Robert B. von Mehren, Chairman of the Special Committee to Study Defender Systems, November 19, 1956.

16. The committee is convinced that the voluntary-defender offices which it has studied attempt to give that scope of representation which the committee believes to be desirable. These voluntary-defender offices have expanded their services whenever it was possible for them to do so and at the same time maintain the quality of their representation.

17. The financial impact of the Bar's dissatisfaction with a voluntary-defender system could be very serious. For example, the New York Legal Aid Society has received approximately one third of its charitable contributions since 1942 from law firms and individual lawyers.

18. This expansion can be illustrated graphically as follows:

COURTS COVERED: DECEMBER 1948

New York County:	*General Sessions; Special Sessions; Magistrates' Court, Felony Part, Youth Term.*
Bronx County:	*Magistrates' Court, Youth Term.*

EXPANSION: 1949–1956

DATE	CRIMINAL COURT
January 1949	*Federal: Southern District*
December 1949	*Kings County: Felony Court*
March 1950	*New York County: Women's Court*
March 1951	*Kings County: Special Sessions*
April 1952	*Bronx County: Felony Court*
September 1954	*Bronx County: Special Sessions*
October 1956	*Federal: Eastern District*

The staff in the Criminal Courts Branch grew from 15 attorneys in 1949 to 24 attorneys by the end of 1957.

19. The background of some of the expansion of the Criminal Courts Branch of the New York Legal Aid Society is discussed by Harrison Tweed in his book, *The Legal Aid Society, New York City, 1876–1951* (1954), at p. 88:

> In 1950 Chief City Magistrate Murtagh requested the Society to supply a staff attorney regularly in the Women's Court, which is the Magistrate's Court handling all cases in which prostitution is charged. The purpose of the request was to rid the court of lawyers hired by the organized vice rings who, together with certain bondsmen, were victimizing many of the girls charged with prostitution. The Society gladly complied with Judge Murtagh's request. About the same time the then Chief Justice of the Court of Special Sessions, Judge Bennett, urged the Society to extend its services to that court in Brooklyn. He secured the signatures of all of the twenty-one judges of his Court, to a letter urging that the Society do this. Accordingly, in March 1951 the Brooklyn office of the Criminal Branch of the Society was reinforced so as to provide this representation in the Court of Special Sessions there. It is unfortunate that Judge Bennett retired before this was done, but his successor, Judge Irving Ben Cooper, is equally enthusiastic and even more energetic.
>
> The last geographical extension of the work of the Criminal Courts Branch was initiated by Judge Murtagh and consisted in the opening of a branch office in the Bronx. This office now provides representation to defendants in the Bronx Arrest Court, which is similar to the Manhattan and Brooklyn Felony Courts. At the opening ceremonies in April 1952 representatives of the Bronx District Attorney's office as well as many judges attended.

20. The Philadelphia Voluntary Defender Association has been constantly concerned with the length of time between arrest and

final disposition for all defendants. It is the firm belief of Mr. Herman Pollock, the Defender, as well as members of the board of directors of the association, that the earlier representation is initiated, the more effective it will be. In this regard the association was instrumental in securing a rule which requires that the police have a defendant arraigned in the Magistrates' Court at the first sitting following arrest. Philadelphia Voluntary Defender Association, *Statement for Community Chest* (Jan. 15, 1955), p. 6; see also *Phila. Dist. Att'y's Office Ann. Rep.* (1952), p. 10. It has been noted that the Voluntary Defender Association does not have the facilities to represent indigent accused in the inferior or Magistrates' Courts. See p. 69, *supra*. For that reason, the period of time between arrest and the initiation of the Voluntary Defender's representation depends upon the speed with which the defendant is transferred to the county jail and requests the services of the Voluntary Defender Association. Once a request has been made, the association conducts its first interview within forty-eight hours—generally before arraignment in the county court. A sampling of 113 cases in which the Voluntary Defender Association appeared in 1956 indicates that the average time between arrest and first interview was 15.5 days.

21. The New Orleans Legal Aid Society initiates its representation in noncapital cases upon the request of a defendant who has been incarcerated in the parish prison. Representation is not provided in inferior courts for two reasons: first, the staff is insufficient to do more than represent those accused in the district or county court; and, second, the criminal procedure in Orleans Parish does not include preliminary examination before a committing magistrate on charges triable in the district court. A defendant, after being arrested and booked in a police station, is transferred directly to the district court for final disposition of his case.

The attorney in charge of the Criminal Branch of the Legal Aid Society of New Orleans estimates that the length of time between arrest and first interview is one month and a half in most noncapital cases. In capital cases, on the other hand, he said that the society will seek to represent the accused prior to his incarceration in the parish prison.

22. There were forty members as of 1957 on the board of directors of the New York Legal Aid Society of which the following were not lawyers:

> *Charles Merz (Chief editorial writer)*
> *The New York Times*
>
> *William H. Miller (Vice-president, bank)*
> *The Hanover Bank*

Robert Montgomery (Actor)

Mrs. Leonard Page Moore (Housewife)

Harold J. Szold (Partner, investment banking firm)
Lehman Brothers

R. Gordon Wasson (Vice-president, bank)
J. P. Morgan & Co., Inc.

Cole J. Younger (Vice-president, bank)
The Chase Manhattan Bank

23. An excellent example is the public-defender system in Alameda County, California. All of the lower committing courts are covered despite their diverse locations. One member of the staff "rides circuit" every day to ensure representation to destitute defendants in the justice of the peace courts in the outlying towns in the county.

24. *Ill. Rev. Stat.*, Ch. 34, §163f (State Bar Ass'n Ed. 1957).

25. *Public Defenders* (Institute of Judicial Administration, New York, May 18, 1956), p. 25.

    The *Report of Junior Section Committee on Indigent Criminal Representation, supra,* note 3, Ch. V, at 245 drew upon the comments of a professor of law who had examined, on a national scale, the work of the various systems utilized to represent indigent criminals. In a letter to the Junior Section Committee, the professor stated: "I was very much struck with the high moral and obvious devotion to duty the public defenders perform, as well as their obvious competence in court. . . ."

26. The committee is advised by the Public Defender of Alameda County, California, that his office has had, for a number of years, the financial resources to prepare fully for trial. Thus, for example, when required his office has sent investigators long distances and has consulted experts and specialists such as psychiatrists, pathologists, ballistics and handwriting experts, interpreters and photographers.

27. At a meeting of the judges of the Superior Court of the State of Connecticut on Monday, June 25, 1956, the following new regulation was adopted: "Public defenders shall not incur any expense for personal services for the investigation of facts prior to trial, or for assistance at trial except the same be approved in advance by the Chief Justice."

28. Approximately 13 students are now available for his use. For a discussion of their work see "From Yale to Jail," 3 (No. 1) Yale L. Rep. (1957), p. 18.

29.   *The Public Defender, upon request of the defendant, or upon order of the Court, shall defend without expense to him, all persons who are not financially able to employ counsel, and who are charged with the commission of any contempt, misdemeanor, felony, or other offense. He shall also, upon request, give counsel and advice to such persons, in and about any charge against them upon which he is conducting the defense, and he shall prosecute all appeals to a higher court or courts, of any person who has been convicted upon any such charge, where, in his opinion, such appeal will, or might reasonably be expected to, result in the reversal or modification of the judgment of conviction.* Charter of the County of Alameda, Cal., §27, as amended, Nov. 2, 1954.

30.   See, *e.g.*, Dimock, "The Public Defender: A Step Towards a Police State?," 42 A. B. A. J. 219 (1956).

31.   One early New York decision, that of *People* v. *Campbell*, 1 Edmonds Select Cas. 307, 307–08 (1846), reported the following colloquy between the Judge and the prisoner at arraignment:

> *The prisoner was indicted for murder, and when arraigned and asked the usual question, whether he demanded a trial? He answered, 'I suppose I am guilty.'*
>
> *Judge—Prisoner, have you counsel?*
>
> *Prisoner—No, sir; I am not able to employ any.*
>
> *Judge—Do you know the difference between murder and manslaughter?*
>
> *Prisoner—No, sir; I only know I struck Cogan with my hod, but I didn't mean to kill him.*
>
> *The judge then ordered the clerk to enter a plea of not guilty, and assigned counsel to defend him.*

In New York in 1886, an attorney assigned to defend an indigent charged with murder sought compensation from the Board of Supervisors. In the course of denying this claim, the court stated:

> *Although at an early day in England, the right of defending by counsel was denied even to a person on trial for the most serious crime, that harsh rule was gradually relaxed until the prisoner became entitled to counsel not only when he was able to employ one, but even when he was not. While the territory now embraced by the State of New York was a colony of Great Britain, it was a part of the common law that counsel should be assigned by the court for the defense of poor persons charged with crime.* People *ex rel.* Brown *v.* Board of Supervisors, 4 N. Y. Crim. Rep. 102, 104 (1886).

32. Beaney, *The Right to Counsel in American Courts* (1955), p. 157.

33. In this connection information contained in Allison and Hassett, "Counsel for the Indigent Defendant," 41 J. Am. Jud. Soc., 102, 104 (1957) and Trebach, "A Modern Defender System for New Jersey," XII Rutgers L. Rev. 289, 315–17 (1957), is also of interest. In their article Allison and Hassett state that in 1956 the city of Baltimore paid more than $56,000 to assigned counsel. Trebach estimates that the cost to the twenty-one counties of New Jersey of fees to assigned counsel in capital cases for the five-year period from 1952 through 1956 reached a total of at least $300,000.

Notes to Chapter VI

1. The rate of recent growth as shown by the fact that the number of central defender offices increased from thirty-eight to eighty-eight between 1951 and 1956. The development of concern for indigents without counsel in criminal courts is also illustrated by increasing judicial demands for their protection and by the amount of new legislation dealing with the problem.

2. The address of the Standing Committee on Legal Aid Work of the American Bar Association and the National Legal Aid and Defender Association are the same: American Bar Center, Chicago 37, Illinois.

3. Brownell, *Legal Aid in the United States* (1951), p. 83.

4. The results of the surveys conducted by the committee's staff may be summarized as follows:

PER CENT OF REPRESENTATION BY CENTRAL DEFENDER
ORGANIZATIONS[a]

	1956	1955	1954	1953	1952
Alameda County Calif. (Superior Court):	57.5%[b]	60.6%[b]			
Legal Aid Society, New York (Court of General Sessions, New York County):		45.8%[c]	45.5%[c]	43.9%[c]	40.4%[c]

	1956	1955	1954	1953	1952
Philadelphia Voluntary Defender (Federal Court):		31.7%[d]	24.%[d]	27.3%[d]	26.9%[d]

Connecticut Public Defenders:[e]

Fairfield County	30.5%[f]
Hartford County	43.2%[g]
New Haven District	37.9%[f]

[a] *This chart should be considered with caution and only as a guide. The defender organizations do not generally tabulate their statistics on the same basis as the courts or the prosecuting offices. In addition, in order to allow more accurate comparison, hearings on violation of probation, habeas corpus applications, motion for re-sentence, etc., and cases in which private counsel were substituted were omitted. Consequently, these figures understate the actual work load of the defender offices involved.*

[b] *7/1–6/30.*

[c] *Calendar year. If cases in which private counsel were substituted are included, percentages for 1955 and 1954 are 55.9% and 55.8% respectively. Note that the New York Legal Aid Society does not handle murder cases. See Appendix.*

[d] *Defenders' year: 6/1–5/31; Federal Statistics: 6/30–7/1. Differences in the method of categorizing cases also make exact comparison impossible.*

[e] *Figures of Probation Department. The figures include only cases processed by the Probation Department.*

[f] *3/1/56–12/31/56.*

[g] *2/1/56–12/31/56.*

5. On August 3, 1953, the Honorable William O. Weissich, District Attorney of Marin County, California, wrote to the Board of Supervisors:

> It has come to my attention that the sum of $15,000.00 has been, or is about to be, budgeted for public defender fees for the fiscal year 1953–54. In my opinion that amount will not be ade-

quate by reason of the fact that the fees in the cases entitled
"People vs. Maggie Hall," "People vs. Burwell and Rogers," and
"People vs. Silva," all of which will be substantial, will be payable
during the current fiscal year.

It is obvious from a review of the Auditor's records that public
defender fees paid out to attorneys appointed by the Courts to
represent indigent defendants have grown constantly and tre-
mendously during the past five or six years, as is demonstrated
by the following figures:

FISCAL YEAR	PUBLIC DEFENDER FEES
1947–1948	$1,850.00
1948–1949	1,950.00
1949–1950	2,550.00
1950–1951	3,727.50
1951–1952	9,100.57
1952–1953	6,996.00

It is true, of course, that the County is reimbursed by the
State Department of Corrections for public defender fees paid
out to attorneys representing inmates of San Quentin Prison.

*   *   *   *   *

Legal authority, therefore, now exists under and by virtue of
which the Board of Supervisors can appoint a public defender
and arrange with the Department of Corrections for a division of
the salary and expenses of such officer on an equitable basis between the County and the Department. In my opinion, there are
available within Marin County many competent attorneys who
would be willing to accept the office of public defender on a part
time basis, for a salary which would be substantially less than the
total amount expected to be paid out during the current year to
Court appointed attorneys. With the salary being equitably ap-
portioned between the County and the Department of Corrections, I believe a substantial saving can be effected not only to the
taxpayers of Marin County but to those of the entire State.

It is instructive to compare with Mr. Weissich's letter the following excerpt from the *Report to the Board of Supervisors for
the Fiscal Year 1955–1956*, by Mr. George Nye, Public Defender of Alameda County, which is a neighbor of Marin County:

In view of these demands upon us, it is fortunate that we
enjoy the advantages of centralization and specialization. For these
reasons, among others, a surprising degree of efficiency has been
achieved. An indication is that in the last fiscal year approximately 6,000 court appearances (A 'court appearance' means no
more than the entry of a lawyer into a courtroom where he

speaks to the court on behalf of a client, whether merely for the entry of a plea, for argument of a motion, or for preliminary examination, trial, sentence or other purpose intended to benefit the defendant's legal position.) were accomplished. The fee schedule of the Alameda County Bar Association provides a minimum fee, in the lowest court, of $50. for each appearance, with substantially higher fees in most situations. If the worth of all the appearances made for our clients were reckoned at this minimum figure, in absolute disregard of the additional value of trial, research, investigation, cases out of court, and screening of applications, the total value of the appearances would still be no less than $300,000. As this department in the last fiscal year expended only $77,373. out of a total budget of $78,540., the members of the office feel that they made an economical as well as useful contribution to the community.

6. See note 1, Ch. V, *supra.*

7.

COSTS OF CENTRAL DEFENDER ORGANIZATIONS EXPRESSED
AS PERCENTAGES OF THE COSTS OF PROSECUTION[a]

Office	1955–6	1954–5	1953–4	Jurisdiction
Philadelphia Voluntary Defender[b, c]	12.2%	11.9%	11.5%	*All cases in County Court and Federal Court except juvenile and capital cases.*
Rochester, New York quasi-Public Defender[b]	6.7%	5.6%		*All cases in Municipal Court, except capital cases.*
Alameda County Public Defender[d]	16.3%	15.5%	14.6%	*All cases: County Court (except Juvenile Court); Municipal Court (Oakland); Justice of the Peace Courts.*
Marin County Public Defender[d]	12.5%	13.3%	6.7%	*All cases in County Court (except Juvenile Court) and felony matters in Municipal Court.*

Office	1955–6	1954–5	1953–4	Jurisdiction
Connecticut				
Public Defenders				
Fairfield	9.8%			*All cases in*
Hartford	9.1%			*Superior Court or*
New Haven*[e]*	16.0%			*Court of Common Pleas.*

a) *This chart should only be used as a guide. The difference in duties, jurisdiction, and fiscal years between the defender offices and prosecution offices prevents exact comparison.*

b) *Since the fiscal year of the defender office differs from the fiscal year of the District Attorney's office exact comparison is impossible.*

c) *The federal prosecutor's costs were not considered.*

d) *The costs of the civil branch of the prosecutor's office were deducted. The fiscal year for Alameda and Marin Counties is from July 1 to June 30.*

e) *Unpaid bills of $1902.30 which were to be paid in the ensuing fiscal year are not included. If they are included, the percentage would be 20.5%.*

8. See pp. 52, 76, *supra.*

9. For example, it has recently been proposed in Massachusetts that legislation be drafted to authorize the payment of public funds to private-defender organizations for service performed in the defense of indigent defendants. See Mass. Bar Assoc., *Interim Report of Special Committee on Counsel for Indigent Defendants,* (February 4, 1957). The Forty-sixth Amendment to the Massachusetts Constitution provides:

Sec. 2. . . . [N]o grant, *appropriation or use of public money or property or loan of public credit shall be made or authorized by the commonwealth or any political division thereof for the purpose of founding, maintaining or aiding . . . any . . . educational, charitable or religious undertaking which is not publicly owned and under the exclusive control, order and superintendence of public officers or public agents authorized by the commonwealth or federal authority or both. . . .*

Sec. 3. *Nothing herein contained shall be construed to prevent the commonwealth . . . from paying to privately controlled hospitals . . . for the deaf, dumb, or blind not more than the ordinary and reasonable compensation for care or support actually rendered or furnished by such hospitals . . . to such persons as may be in whole or in part unable to support or care for themselves.*

Section 2 would seem to prohibit the enactment of legislation of the type proposed. Even though the exception provided by Section 3 has been interpreted as not restricted to per capita payments to hospitals for the deaf, dumb, and blind, a report recently prepared by the Harvard Defenders Committee states that, on the basis of past opinions of the Attorney General of Massachusetts, per capita payments to private defender organizations would be unconstitutional.

10. The effect of business upon the practice of law in one large city has been said to be this:

> *Our lawyers have been swallowed up by business, absorbed by its requirements and engrossed in its problems, as it has grown and expanded year by year. Very few are interested or qualified in criminal practice. And in the transition a greater cleavage has taken place between civil and criminal practice. Criminal administration has continued substantially the same. In civil practice each of the various special branches has developed into a vocation in itself.* Mathews, "The Disappearing Landmark—Defense of Indigent Criminals," 27 N.Y.S.B. Bull. 403–04 (1955).

Despite this cleavage between civil and criminal practice, community responsibility for the indigent accused should begin with the legal profession. It is the lawyer's familiarity with, and concern for, a fair administration of justice which should prompt the development of adequate standards of representation. His knowledge and awareness make it desirable for him to participate in the community's supervision of the system in operation. A majority of the members of the boards of directors of voluntary-defender organizations are attorneys.

11. One of the sources of public pressure is the defense of the unpopular cause. An interesting example occurred in Boston in 1955. The Voluntary Defenders Committee, Inc. of Boston was criticized in a newspaper article for representing individuals who had been charged with shooting a policeman. The article, "This Is How I See It," by W. E. Mullins, The Boston Herald, May 12, 1955, stated:

> *Perhaps the Legislature should look into this public defenders situation and have the state take it over, if only to prevent slick criminals from getting their convictions up to Supreme Court on grounds of inadequate defence. It certainly should not be a function of the Red Feather. Contributors to this laudable agency of mercy don't give to help hoodlums like those who shot Officer Connolly, even on the civil rights dodge.*

Needless to say, this committee cannot agree in any respect with Mr. Mullins' position.

12. Kelley, "How Now New York," LV (No. 1) The Legal Aid Review 15, 19 (1957).

13. Nye, "The Glass-Bottomed Boat," LV (No. 1) The Legal Aid Review 7, 13–14 (1957).

    A recent study of the Public Defender's operation in Cook County, Illinois was conducted by a subcommittee of the Chicago Bar Association. This subcommittee recommended, *inter alia*, the following:

    2. *A permanent committee of The Chicago Bar Association should be appointed to assist the Cook County Public Defender.*

    A. *The name of this committee should be the* Public Defender Committee. *The membership of the Committee should include: the Public Defender; the Chief Justice of the Criminal Court of Cook County or some other Judge designated by him; members of the Defense of Prisoners Committee; and other members of The Chicago Bar Association.*

    B. *The functions of this committee should be:*

        (1) *To advise and aid the Public Defender in formulating the policies of his office; (2) To aid the Public Defender in preparing his budget and in securing funds; (3) To interview prospective assistant Public Defenders, and to recommend applicants to the Public Defenders, and to the Executive Committees of the Judges; (4) To correlate the activities of the Public Defender with other committees of the association, such as the Defense of Prisoners, Criminal Law, and Public Information Committees; (5) To initiate a program whereby third year law students could gain experience by assisting the Public Defender's Office.*

    C. *Finally, this committee should have a Sub-Committee consisting of a few members to undertake a study of the Public Defender system and recommend basic changes for its improvement, or if necessary, its elimination.* Chicago Bar Association, *Report of the Sub-committee Appointed to Study the Report and Recommendations of the Joint Committee On Legal Aid And Defense of Prisoners,* (November 28, 1956).

14. See pp. 87-88, *infra.*

15. See pp. 60-61, *supra.*

16. See p. 61, *supra.*

17. Dimock, "The Public Defender: A Step Towards a Police State?," 42 A. B. A. J. 219, 220 (1956).

18. In this connection note the following Colorado statute:

    Students of any law school which has been continuously in existence for at least ten years prior to the passage of this section and which maintains a legal aid dispensary where poor persons receive legal advice and services, shall when representing said dispensary and its clients and then only be authorized to appear in court as if licensed to practice. Col. Rev. Stat. Ann. *1953, Ch. 12, Art. 1, §19.*

19. See Scull, "Voluntary Defenders Aid Many Indigent Prisoners," 22 (No. 2) Harv. L. Record 4 (1956).

20. See pp. 52, 76, *supra.*

21. The Report of the Subcommittee of the Chicago Bar Association, *supra*, Ch. VI, note 13, recommended the amendment of the Illinois statute which restricts the jurisdictions of the Public Defender. The recommendation read:

    Section 4 of the Public Defender Act (Ch. 34, §163 (f), Ill. Rev. Stat. 1955), which restricts the Public Defender to Courts of record, exercising a general criminal jurisdiction within the county, should be amended to permit the Public Defender to appear and represent indigents in all courts and through all stages of the proceedings.

22. See pp. 74-75, *supra.*

23. The committee is impressed with the results obtained by the civil service approach in Alameda County, California. In that jurisdiction the Public Defender and his assistants must take both a written and an oral examination. The names of the three applicants who receive the highest grades in the examination for the position of Public Defender are submitted to the Board of Supervisors of the County for final selection. In the case of assistants, the choice is left to the Public Defender himself. It is believed that the Public Defender thereby gains a position of independence and strength which increases his effectiveness.

Note to Chapter VII

1. Hughes, "Legal Aid Societies, Their Function and Necessity," *Report of the Forty-Third Annual Meeting of the American Bar Association* (1920), p. 234.

Notes to Appendix

1. This chart is designed to present the salient features of the statutory provisions of forty-eight states (the new state of Alaska is not included) pertaining to the assignment of counsel for indigent defendants in criminal cases. Since the chart is necessarily condensed, reference must be made to the citations and the cases in order to develop a thorough picture of any state. In addition, in the interest of brevity, this chart does not include certain provisions relating to the assignment of counsel which may involve criminal matters. For example, no reference has been made to the provisions relating to extradition. Many of the states have adopted the uniform extradition law, in whole or in part, and may have included those provisions relating to the assignment of counsel. In addition, no reference has been made to Juvenile Compact Laws which may also provide for the appointment of counsel or to provisions relating to the assignment of counsel for those charged with being criminally insane or sexual psychopaths.

2. Trial judge may call upon any "welfare agency" to investigate and report on the truth of the petitioner's verified statement of indigency. *Ala. Code* 1940, Title 15, §382 (4).

3. Note that counsel must also be appointed upon insanity hearings. Such counsel receive reasonable compensation within courts discretion. *Ariz. Rev. Stat. Ann.* 1956, §§36–507, 13–1673, 13–1721.

4. A plea of guilty in Magistrates' Court to a felony charge cannot be accepted unless defendant is represented by counsel. *Cal. Pen. Code,* §859a.

5. Automatic appeal from death sentence.

6. All counties have public defenders.

7. Public Defender in Broward County by Private Act, and in Dade County.

8. Before receiving compensation the assigned attorney must file an affidavit indicating the compensation, if any, he has received or will receive from any source. *Ga. Code Ann.* 1947, §27–3003.

9. Art. 1, §1, ¶5 of the Georgia Constitution, §2–105 of the Georgia Code, has been construed as follows:

   Our courts have given the . . . provisions of the constitution (above) a very liberal construction, a construction which in effect places upon the judge presiding at the trial of one charged with a criminal offense the affirmative duty of seeing to it that the defendant is represented by counsel. Where the defendant is

*unable to employ counsel, the court must appoint one for him,
if he desires it. . . . Accordingly, it has been the . . . practice for
the trial judge to inquire of the defendant if he has employed
counsel, or if he is able to do so, and, if not, whether he desires
the court to appoint one for him. . . .* Harris v. Norris, 188 Ga.
610, 611, 4 S.E. 2d 840, 842 (1939). See also *Bibb County* v.
Hancock, 211 Ga. 429, 86 S.E. 2d 511 (1945); *McGhee* v. *State,*
72 Ga. App. 52, 30 S.E. 2d 54 (1955); *Rowland* v. *State,* 72 Ga.
App. 793, 35 S.E. 2d 372, *app. transferred,* 199 Ga. 340, 34 S.E.
2d 577 (1945).

10. It would seem that the trial judge must appoint counsel for an
    indigent defendant upon request regardless of the permissive
    language of the statute. See *State* v. *Eikelberger,* 70 Idaho 271,
    215 P. 2d 996 (1950).

11. A defendant charged with being an habitual criminal is to be in-
    formed of "his right to counsel at such hearing." *Ill. Ann. Stats.
    (1957),* Ch. 38, §603.3.

12. The jurisdiction of the Public Defender is dependent on the size
    of the county. In addition, where the Public Defender has juris-
    diction, the court, with the assent of the defendant may, and
    upon request of the defendant must, appoint other counsel. *Id.,*
    Ch. 34, §163f.

13. The Constitution of Indiana has been construed as follows:
    ". . . it is the duty of the court to select a competent attorney
    for him at public expense whether he requests it or not. There
    can be no valid trial of a criminal case unless a defendant is rep-
    resented by counsel, if he desires counsel." *State* v. *Minton,*
    234 Ind. 578, 581, 130 N.E. 2d 226, 228 (1955).

14. Assigned counsel would appear to be entitled to compensation
    regardless of any legislative provision therefor and regardless
    whether funds have been appropriated for such purpose. *Knox
    County Counsel* v. *State* ex rel. *McCormick,* 217 Ind. 493, 29
    N.E. 2d 405 (1940).

15. Iowa also provides for the mandatory appointment of counsel for
    those charged with being sexual psychopaths. *Iowa Code Ann.*
    1946, §225A.5.

16. Apart from the narrow provision of §455.010 the right to counsel
    has stemmed from judicial interpretation of the constitution of
    the Commonwealth of Kentucky. See *Hart* v. *Commonwealth,*
    296 S.W. 2d 212 (1956).

17. Voluntary Defender in Orleans Parish.

18. *Pike* v. *State,* 152 Me. 83, 123 A 2d 774 (1956). See re insane
    Me. Rev. Stat. Ann. 1954, Ch. 27, §123.

19. Counsel must be appointed in hearing on charge that defendant is a defective delinquent. *Md. Code Ann.* 1957, Art. 318, §8.

20. There are voluntary-defender offices in Boston and Springfield which service a number of counties.

21. §28.1253 as amended would seem to allow the court in its discretion to appoint counsel upon preliminary examination.

22. Public Defenders in Hennepin and Ramsey counties receive salaries.

23. *Robinson v. State*, 178 Miss. 568, 173 So. 451 (1937).

24. Public Defender for City of St. Louis per city ordinance. Note that counsel may be appointed on hearing in sexual psychopath cases. *Mo. Stat. Ann.* 1953, §202.720.

25. Public Defender in Douglas County.

26. In noncapital cases, it is discretionary with the appellate court whether counsel should be assigned on appeal when trial minutes are available to the defendant. *People v. Kalan*, 2 N.Y. 2d 278, 140 N.E. 2d 357 (1957); *People v. Breslin*, 4 N.Y. 2d 73, 149 N.E. 2d 85 (1958). Voluntary Defender in New York City. Mixed Public and Private Defender in Erie and Monroe counties.

27. In re *Taylor*, 230 N.C. 566, 53, S.E. 2d 857 (1949).

28. Public Defender in Columbus and Voluntary Defender in Hamilton County.

29. Public Defenders in Tulsa and Oklahoma counties receive salary.

30. Voluntary Defenders in Allegheny and Philadelphia counties.

31. Public Defender in Shelby County.

32. In *Lynch v. Republic*, 4 Wash. 2d 379, 243 P. 2d 636 (1952), the court stated that there was no requirement to inform a defendant of his right to counsel in municipal court since prosecution was not by indictment or information.

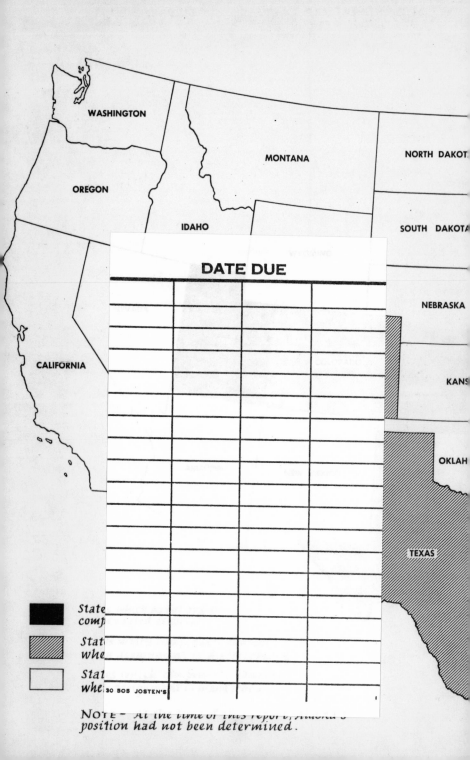

WASHINGTON

MONTANA

NORTH DAKOT

OREGON

IDAHO

SOUTH DAKOTA

NEBRASKA

CALIFORNIA

KANS

OKLAH

TEXAS

DATE DUE

30 505 JOSTEN'S

State
comp

Stat
whe

Stat
whe

NOTE- At the time of this report, Alaska's
position had not been determined.